T0059879

What is
Medieval History?
Second Edition

What is History? series

Peter Burke, *What is Cultural History?* 2nd edition
Peter Burke, *What is the History of Knowledge?*
John C. Burnham, *What is Medical History?*
Pamela Kyle Crossley, *What is Global History?*
Pero Gaglo Dagbovie, *What is African American History?*
Shane Ewen, *What is Urban History?*
Christiane Harzig and Dirk Hoerder, with Donna Gabaccia,
    What is Migration History?
J. Donald Hughes, *What is Environmental History?* 2nd
    edition
Andrew Leach, *What is Architectural History?*
Stephen Morillo with Michael F. Pavkovic, *What is Military
    History?* 3rd edition
James Raven, *What is the History of the Book?*
Sonya O. Rose, *What is Gender History?*
Barbara H. Rosenwein and Riccardo Cristiani, *What is the
    History of Emotions?*
Hannu Salmi, *What is Digital History?*
Brenda E. Stevenson, *What is Slavery?*
Jeffrey Weeks, *What is Sexual History?*
Richard Whatmore, *What is Intellectual History?*
Merry E. Wiesner-Hanks, *What is Early Modern History?*

What is Medieval History?

Second Edition

John H. Arnold

polity

Copyright © John H. Arnold 2021

The right of John H. Arnold to be identified as Author of this Work has been asserted in accordance with the UK Copyright, Designs and Patents Act 1988.

First published in 2008 by Polity Press
This edition published in 2021 by Polity Press

Polity Press
65 Bridge Street
Cambridge CB2 1UR, UK

Polity Press
101 Station Landing
Suite 300
Medford, MA 02155, USA

ISBN-13: 978-1-5095-3255-1
ISBN-13: 978-1-5095-3256-8(pb)

A catalogue record for this book is available from the British Library.

Library of Congress Cataloging-in-Publication Data
Names: Arnold, John, 1969- author.
Title: What is medieval history? / John H. Arnold.
Description: Second edition. | Medford, MA : Polity Press, 2021. | Series:
    What is history? | Includes bibliographical references and index. |
    Summary: "A rich and compelling overview of the sources and methods used
    by medieval historians"-- Provided by publisher.
Identifiers: LCCN 2020013070 (print) | LCCN 2020013071 (ebook) | ISBN
    9781509532551 (hardback) | ISBN 9781509532568 (paperback) | ISBN
    9781509532582 (epub)
Subjects: LCSH: Middle Ages. | Middle Ages--Study and teaching. |
    Medievalists.
Classification: LCC D117 .A72 2020 (print) | LCC D117 (ebook) | DDC
    940.1072--dc23
LC record available at https://lccn.loc.gov/2020013070
LC ebook record available at https://lccn.loc.gov/2020013071

Typeset in 10.5 on 12 pt Sabon by
Servis Filmsetting Ltd, Stockport, Cheshire
Printed and bound in Great Britain by CPI Group (UK) Ltd, Croydon

The publisher has used its best endeavours to ensure that the URLs for external websites referred to in this book are correct and active at the time of going to press. However, the publisher has no responsibility for the websites and can make no guarantee that a site will remain live or that the content is or will remain appropriate.

Every effort has been made to trace all copyright holders, but if any have been overlooked the publisher will be pleased to include any necessary credits in any subsequent reprint or edition.

For further information on Polity, visit our website: politybooks.com

This one is for Alex

Contents

Illustrations

Preface to the Second Edition

The primary purpose in producing a second edition is to include some new and additional material that relates to methods and debates that have become more prominent over the decade-and-a-bit since I wrote the original book. This mainly consists of expansions to sections within Chapter 3, and a new section on 'Globalisms' in Chapter 4. As the original introduction admits, 'my coverage tends towards western Europe', and this is still the case; but the original did already reach out to a wider geography on occasion, and I have here attempted to expand upon that enlarged sense of 'the medieval'.

I have also taken the opportunity to amend the text in minor ways in some other places, for greater clarity of expression and to include some additional examples where they are particularly illuminating. As with the original book, I remain deeply indebted to a host of colleagues and their work for my understanding of the middle ages; I should note, in particular, conversations with Ulf Büntgen, Matthew Collins, Pat Geary, Caroline Goodson, Monica Green, Eyal Poleg and Peter Sarris regarding recent work in science and archaeology. I am grateful to Pascal Porcheron at Polity for prompting my further work, and for the careful labours of Ellen MacDonald-Kramer, Sarah Dancy and others involved in its production. This second edition remains a work that aims to introduce 'the medieval', not in any sense claiming fully to represent it, or the fullness of its study.

Preface and Acknowledgements

This is a book about what historians of the middle ages do, rather than a history of the middle ages itself, though it will also provide a sense of that period. Each chapter focuses on a different aspect of the historian's task, and the conditions of its possibility. Chapter 1 discusses the idea of 'the middle ages' and its associations, and the foundational contours of academic medievalism. Chapter 2 looks at sources, the possibilities and problems that they present to the historian. Chapter 3 examines intellectual tools which medievalists have borrowed from other subject areas, and the insights they provide. Chapter 4 tries to indicate the shape of some key and broad-ranging discussions in current historiography. The final chapter addresses the very purpose of medieval history – its present and potential roles, in academic debate and society more broadly. The book is written neither as a blankly 'objective' report on the field, nor as a polemical call to arms, but as an engaged survey which seeks to both explain and comment upon the wider discipline. In what follows, I assume some knowledge of, and interest in, history on the reader's part, but little prior sense of the medieval period (roughly the years 500–1500). Rather than always listing particular centuries, I have sometimes made use of the loose division of the medieval period into 'early', 'high' and 'late'. All that is meant by this is $c.500–c.1050$, $c.1050–c.1300$ and $c.1300–c.1500$. My coverage tends towards western Europe, but I have tried to indicate the greater breadth of medievalism that exists beyond; to do more would take a much bigger book.

I am indebted to various people in my attempt to chart, in so few pages, so large an area. Rob Bartlett, Mark Ormrod and Richard Kieckhefer all kindly answered particular queries at key moments. Rob Liddiard and Caroline Goodson helped me understand aspects of archaeology, Sophie Page did similarly with regard to magic and David Wells assisted my grasp of Wolfram von Eschenbach. Major thanks are due to those who very generously read and commented on individual chapters or indeed the whole book: two anonymous readers for Polity, Cordelia Beattie, Caroline Goodson, Victoria Howell, Matt Innes, Geoff Koziol and Christian Liddy; Matt and Geoff also kindly shared unpublished material with me. Any errors are entirely my own fault. Thanks are owed also to Andrea Drugan at Polity, for prompting me to write the book and for being an understanding editor during the process. As ever, I am grateful to Victoria and Zoë for giving me the support and the space in which to write.

Lastly, this book is dedicated to all those who have taught me how to teach, from my parents, Henry and Hazel Arnold, to my students past and present.

Map of Europe, *c.*900

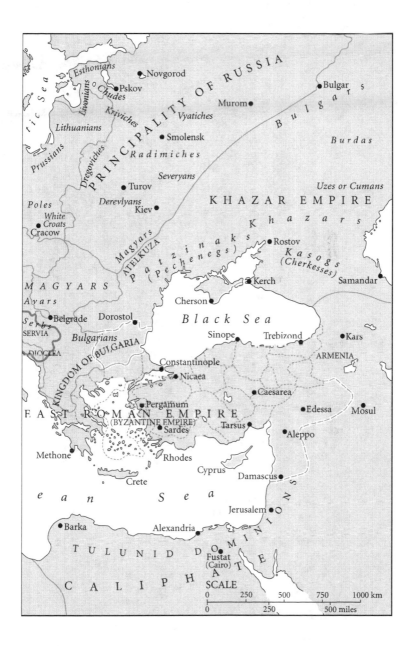

PRINCIPALITY OF RUSSIA

tic Sea

Esthonians
Chudes
• Pskov
• Novgorod
Livonians
Kriviches
Vyatiches
Murom •
• Bulgar s
Bulgar s
Lithuanians
• Smolensk
Burdas
Prussians
Radimiches
Dregoviches
Severyans
Poles
• Turov
Derevlyans
KHAZAR EMPIRE
Uzes or Cumans
White
Croats
• Kiev
K h a z a r s
Cracow
Magyars
ATELKUZA
Patzinaks
(Pechenegs)
• Rostov
Kasogs
(Cherkesses)
MAGYARS
Samandar
Avars
• Kerch
Cherson •
Black Sea
Serbs
• Belgrade
Dorostol •
SERVIA
Bulgarians
Sinope •
Trebizond •
• Kars
DIOCLEA
KINGDOM OF BULGARIA
Constantinople •
ARMENIA
• Nicaea
EAST ROMAN EMPIRE
• Caesarea
(BYZANTINE EMPIRE)
• Edessa
Mosul •
Pergamum
Sardes
Tarsus •
• Aleppo
Methone
Rhodes
Cyprus
Damascus •
Crete
e a n
S e a
Jerusalem •
• Barka
Alexandria
T U L U N I D
D O M I N I O N S
Fustat
(Cairo)
C A L I P H A T E
SCALE

0   250   500   750   1000 km

0   250   500 miles

SCALE

| 0 | 250 | 500 | 750 | 1000 km |

| 0 | 250 | 500 miles |

ATLANTIC
OCEAN

NORWAY

S o W

Stockholm

GOTHLAND

SCOTLAND

Edinburgh

*North
Sea*

DENMARK

Copenhagen

IRELAND

Dublin

York

Lübeck POMERANIA

Bremen BRANDENBURG Posen

ENGLAND

Magdeburg LUSATIA SILESIA

London

Ponthieu Calais BRABANT HOLY

Leipzig

BRITTANY

LUXEMBOURG ROMAN Prague

Paris Reims Treves BOHEMIA

KINGDOM EMPIRE MORAVIA

OF Augsburg BAVARIA Vienna

Poitiers AUSTRIA

DUCHY FRANCE TYROL STYRIA

Bordeaux OF Lyons Geneva CARINTHIA Trieste

AQUITAINE DAUPHINE LANDS OF CROATIA

Santiago VISCONTI

Leon PROVENCE Genoa BOSNIA

NAVARRE Toulouse PAPAL

Saragossa *Marseilles* STATES

KINGDOM ARAGON Siena

Lisbon OF Barcelona Corsica Rome

PORTUGAL Toledo

CASTILE Sardinia Naples

Seville KINGDOM

Granada *Balearic Is* OF NAPLES

GRANADA *M e d i t e r* Palermo

KINGDOM

OF SICILY

MOROCCO ALGERIA Tunis *r* Malta

n

TUNIS *e*

Tripoli

TRIPOLI

Boundary of the Holy Roman Empire
Lands of the Habsburgs
Lands of the House of Bohemia and Luxembourg
Eastern Empire
Dominions of Edward III in 1360
French Royal Domain
Church Lands
Boundary of the Dominions of Stephen Dushan (1331–55)

Map of Europe, *c*.1360

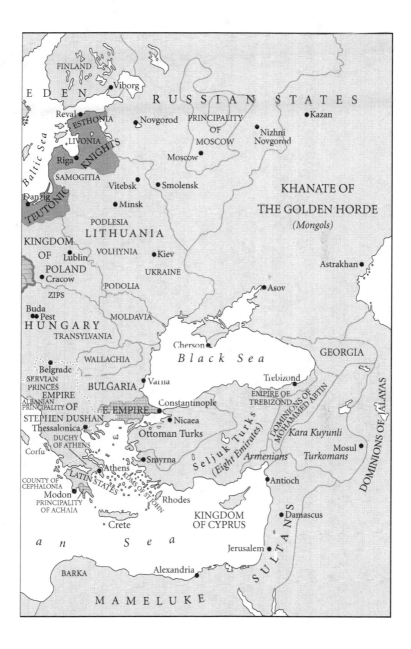

FINLAND

Viborg

E D E N

R U S S I A N   S T A T E S

Reval

ESTHONIA

LIVONIA

KNIGHTS

Baltic Sea

Riga

SAMOGITIA

Danzig

TEUTONIC

Novgorod

PRINCIPALITY
OF
MOSCOW

Moscow

Kazan

Nizhni
Novgorod

KHANATE OF

THE GOLDEN HORDE

(Mongols)

Vitebsk

Smolensk

Minsk

PODLESIA

L I T H U A N I A

KINGDOM
OF
POLAND

Lublin

VOLHYNIA

Kiev

Astrakhan

Cracow

UKRAINE

ZIPS

PODOLIA

Buda
Pest

MOLDAVIA

Asov

H U N G A R Y

TRANSYLVANIA

Cherson

B l a c k   S e a

GEORGIA

Belgrade

WALLACHIA

SERVIAN
PRINCES
EMPIRE

BULGARIA

Varna

Trebizond

ALBANIAN
PRINCIPALITY OF
STEPHEN DUSHAN

E. EMPIRE

Constantinople

EMPIRE OF
TREBIZOND

DOMINIONS OF
MOHAMMED ABTIN

DOMINIONS OF JALAYAS

Thessalonica

Nicaea

DUCHY
OF ATHENS

Corfu

Ottoman Turks

Kara Kuyunli

Athens

Smyrna

Seljuk Turks

(Eight Emirates)

Armenians

Mosul
Turkomans

LATIN STATES

KING OF ST. JOHN

COUNTY OF
CEPHALONIA

Antioch

Modon

PRINCIPALITY
OF ACHAIA

Rhodes

KINGDOM
OF CYPRUS

Damascus

a n   *S e a*

Crete

Jerusalem

SULTANS

BARKA

Alexandria

M A M E L U K E

1

Framing the Middle Ages

A Medieval Tale

The first time Bartolomeo the priest talked to them was on 9 February 1320, in the papal palace at Avignon, and his interrogation probably took up most of one day. A notary, Gerard, wrote down his words; thus they survive for us today. Three very powerful men – a cardinal, an abbot from Toulouse and the pope's legate for northern Italy – questioned, listened and re-questioned.

Matters had begun, Bartolomeo explained, the previous year, in October. A letter had arrived from Matteo Visconti, duke of Milan, summoning the priest to his presence. And so Bartolomeo had obeyed.

He met with the Visconti conspirators (he explained to his interrogators) in a room in Matteo's palace. Scoto de San Gemignano, a judge, was there, as was a physician, Antonio Pelacane. Initially, Matteo drew him to one side. He told the priest that 'he wished to do Bartolomeo a great service, benefit and honour, and that he wished that Bartolomeo would do Matteo a great service, indeed the greatest, namely the greatest that anyone living could do for him; and Matteo added that he knew for certain that Bartolomeo knew well how to do the aforesaid service of which Matteo was thinking.' He would do whatever he could, Bartolomeo protested.

Immediately Matteo called to Scoto, the judge, telling him to show Bartolomeo what he had with him. 'Then the said lord Scoto drew out from his robe and held out and showed to Bartholomeo and Matteo a certain silver image, longer than the palm of a hand, in the figure of a man: members, head, face, arms, hands, belly, thighs, legs, feet and natural organs.' Written on the front of the statue were these words: *Jacobus papa Johannes*, 'Jacques pope John'. The present pope, John XXII, had been called Jacques d'Euze before taking the pontifical title.

This was not the only thing written on the image. There was a sign, like a reversed 'N', and a name: *Amaymo*. The name of a demon.

'Bartolomeo, behold this image,' said Matteo, 'which I have made to bring destruction to the pope who persecutes me.' What Matteo wanted of Bartolomeo was for the priest to help finish the magical object, by suffusing the image with incense from *zuccum de mapello* ('What is *zuccum de mapello*?' asked Bartolomeo's interrogators in Avignon, some months later. A kind of poison, he explained. But, he emphasized, he did not want to go along with Matteo's plan).[1]

Bartolomeo told Matteo that he had no *zuccum de mapello*, and was unable to help. He then left, threatened by the duke to keep silent. But some time later Scoto came to see him, to ask his advice on the details of some books of sorcery. Prompted by Bartolomeo, Scoto again showed him the statue. It had been finished by a different sorceror from Verona, and was inscribed with a new word, *Meruyn*. All that now need happen, Scoto explained, was to hang the statue up for seventy-two nights, placing it night after night in a fire. As, little by little, the fire consumed the image, so would its target, little by little, be destroyed.

And that was all he knew, Bartolomeo explained to the cardinal, the abbot, the legate and the scribe. He had come to Avignon to warn Pope John XXII that his life was in danger.

But that was not the end of it, because some months later, on 11 September 1320, Bartolomeo was once again before this gathering of interrogators, explaining what had happened to him in the intervening period. When he had returned to Milan the previous March, he said, he had immediately been arrested and brought before Scoto. The Milanese knew that he had been to Avignon, and suspected that he had revealed the plot concerning the statue. He was imprisoned, in chains, for weeks. Scoto came to interrogate him many times. Bartolomeo told him that he'd gone to Avignon to treat a sick man, a knight who was under a magical curse. Scoto did not believe him. Matteo was very angry with him, Scoto explained; it would be better to confess now. 'Come, Bartolomeo, tell the truth, why you went to the Curia', Scoto said at one time. 'Because you know absolutely that in the end it will happen that you tell the truth; and if you will not speak courteously, you will end up speaking under torture. Although I want you to know that I do not want to place you in torment, however in the end it will have to be, that you are tortured, unless you spontaneously wish to say the truth.' Bartolomeo stuck with his story.

And he was tortured. Stripped, his hands tied behind him to a stick, a heavy stone was placed on his legs, while Scoto's assistants yanked his arms back. They pulled him up, then released him, pulled him up, then released him. He was then untied, and led back to his cell. Look, said Scoto, we can do this to you every night. Every night until you die. Just confess.

But Bartolomeo did not confess. What saved him eventually was the intervention of another powerful northern duke, Galeazzo Visconti, Matteo's son. Galeazzo had him freed, apologized for what had happened, hoped that he was all right. But Galeazzo was also in on the plot, and inveigled Bartolomeo into helping once again: the statue must be freshly suffused, and Bartolomeo was the man to do it – by implication, a proof of Bartolomeo's loyalties. And by implication, prison, torture and death the alternative. Let me think about it, Bartolomeo pleaded. Very well, said Galeazzo; but 'you should know that I have had Master Dante Alighieri come to me regarding this matter that I'm asking of you.' Good, said Bartolomeo: I would be very pleased if he did what you are asking. But no: Galeazzo really doesn't want to ask Dante to do it – because he knows that Bartolomeo can do it, will do it.

Two days later Bartolomeo agreed, set about finding more *zuccum de mapello*, and retrieved the statue from Galeazzo. He returned with it to his home town – and then he fled to Avignon once more.

And where is the statue?, asked his interrogators. I brought it with me, Bartolomeo replied. He produced a bundle tied with twine, unwrapped it, and drew out a silver figure in the shape of a man. And it was just exactly as he had described it, as the interrogators attested for the written record.[2]

There the story ends, Bartolomeo's story at any rate. The struggles between John XXII and the Visconti continued for some time, and other witnesses raised against them describe their impiety, their heresy, their usury and other crimes. The pope believed himself subject to further magical attacks, and encouraged inquisitors to be on the lookout for sorcery. The Visconti themselves survived as a family for a long time, ruling Milan late into the fifteenth century without break. But of Bartolomeo the priest we know nothing more.

At first sight this is what one might call a very medieval tale. It involves tyrants, a pope, intrigue, torture and magical practices of a kind now usually described as 'superstitious'. We may have a fairly vivid mental image of some of the more lurid parts of the story, not least because this kind of middle ages has inspired (directly or indirectly) various aspects of modern culture. Film, television, novels and comics have pictured a dark, grubby, bloody middle ages: *The Name of the Rose*, *Braveheart* or the various films about Joan of Arc, for example. There is a similar template for future barbarism: *Mad Max*, *Robocop* and *The Hunger Games* (Katniss Everdeen having distant kinship with Robin Hood) all bear the imprint of a certain kind of medievalism. 'I'm gonna get medieval on yo' ass', as Marcellus Wallace threatens his erstwhile torturers in *Pulp Fiction*. George R. R. Martin's *Game of Thrones* famously replays the horrors of late medieval politics with added sex and dragons. So, in one sense, Bartolomeo's experiences are familiar.

But there is more here than immediately meets the eye. Matteo Visconti's plot against the pope may look typically 'medieval', but it contains elements that, on reflection, may surprise us. And it sits at an intersection of themes, lives, geographies and forces that are far more complex – and interesting – than those stereotyped depictions, which Umberto Eco once called 'the shaggy middle ages', would suggest.[3] Take magic. Everyone 'knows' that the middle ages was a superstitious age, full of witches, demons, spells and the suppression of the same by the Inquisition. But the magic in this story is located not where we might expect to find it: not in the simple hut stuck at the end of the village, inhabited by a poor widow and her cat, but in learned Latin books, read and owned by clerics, right at the heart of the city and intellectual culture. This was not in fact unusual: while healers and soothsayers were found in rural medieval parishes, the kind of magic described here was very much a clerical subculture, available only to those with a Latin education. The roots of this magic were not 'pagan' in the sense of pre-Christian primitivism; nor was it, within medieval terms, a set of irrational ideas. Learned magic derived in part from classical scholarship, in part from ideas about hidden ('occult') natural forces and in part from a long tradition of Christian theology, which saw demons as constantly present – and, in certain circumstances, harnessable to good or bad ends. Learned magic and science were intimately connected, and would continue to be for several centuries to come.

Nor were ecclesiastical attitudes to this magic always quite what one might expect. The Inquisition did not automatically pursue its practitioners, not least because there was no such thing as the 'Inquisition' in the sense of a permanent and central tribunal until the mid-sixteenth century (with the exception of Spain, where the Spanish Inquisition began under secular direction in 1480). While inquisitors into heretical depravity were appointed directly by the papacy, their practical powers were largely dependent upon the cooperation of secular authorities in any particular area. Furthermore, local bishops, parochial priests and monastic orders could have different ideas from inquisitors and the papacy about desirable orthodox practice and the demands of the faith. The 'Church' was a complex and in some ways wildly heterogeneous edifice. The procedures that were used when interrogating Bartolomeo were inquisitorial in the sense of being a legal technique, and one could describe the cardinal, abbot and legate as 'inquisitors' only while they were engaged in interviewing the priest. Torture was involved in our story, but although it had indeed been permitted since 1252 in heresy trials, in this case, as we saw, it was the secular authorities in Milan that tortured poor Bartolomeo.

In any case, Bartolomeo's tale is not a story about magic at all. It is really about politics and communication. Despite all the evidence alleged against them, nothing happened to Matteo or Galeazzo Visconti, because the pope simply didn't have the power to touch them. The very reason that John XXII was in Avignon rather than Rome was that northern Italy had become too politically fraught for him to stay there (the papacy had moved to Avignon in 1309, through a combination of pressure from the French monarchy and factional political fighting in Rome; there it remained until 1377). If the Visconti were attempting to assassinate the pope, it was because of political matters: a few years before Bartolomeo's reports, John XXII had been attempting to stop conflict between Milan, Brescia and Sicily. Matteo Visconti had agreed to the terms of a peace treaty, but the pope had then, in March 1317, declared that Ludwig of Bavaria held the title of Holy Roman Emperor illegally. Since the Visconti based their right to rule Milan on claims of a past imperial appointment, this threw them back into conflict with the papacy and Milan's neighbours; and in 1318 Matteo was excommunicated. In theory, excommunication was a very serious matter: one was removed from the community of the Christian faithful, denied the sacraments and, unless reconciled before death, denied entry into heaven. But John XXII had been a little too lavish in his use of excommunication as a political weapon, and contemporary commentators were quite clear that the political struggles going on were nothing to do with matters of faith.

So much for the politics (the complexities of which, if further explicated, could easily fill this entire book and a shelf full more). What of communication? Several forms and facets were apparent in Bartolomeo's tale, not least the very document in which it was recorded. Inquisition was a highly textual form of inquiry, and the rich details given above – all of which are drawn directly from the evidence – demonstrate in themselves the development of a particular kind of written technology. The magic being discussed was written magic, and although this was innately arcane and specialized, the existence of books and written documents in general was far from rare. A northern Italian city such as Milan was by this period a highly literate society: some estimates suggest that the majority of adults in this kind of milieu could read and write in the vernacular. This was admittedly the likely pinnacle of medieval literacy; in other countries, in rural areas and in earlier centuries, access to texts would sometimes have been much more limited. But mechanisms of communication were always more complex than a stereotyped picture of the middle ages would suggest. As we have already seen, matters of local, national and international politics involved the flow of information across Europe. Even in the countryside, villages might well have a notary who could act as the conduit for written information. And it was not only documents that could bring news, but also people. Bartolomeo travelled with relative ease between Milan and Avignon; the Visconti were capable (presumably through spies) of discovering where he had been in advance of his return. Trade routes linked together various European centres, and indeed connected Europe to the Middle East and North Africa (a topic to which we shall return in a later chapter). Letters, reports, recorded interrogations, archives, sermons, songs, stories and images all circulated across European kingdoms. It was not as information-rich an age as the twenty-first century; but neither was it as isolated or ignorant as is often assumed.

For much of the middle ages, writing was seen as an artisanal skill, something that highly intellectual authors would not stoop to perform themselves; they would, rather, dictate their works to a scribe. Someone like Bartolomeo would have thought of himself as 'literate' (*litteratus*), but by this he would have meant particularly that he could read Latin rather than the vernacular, and that through reading Latin he was steeped in the wisdom and traditions of Christian intellectual thought. One could be fluent in writing a vernacular language – as, for example, many merchants would have been – and yet still be seen as *illitteratus*, lacking in Latin. However, at this very time and place, such conceptions were being challenged by a marginal figure in Bartolomeo's story: Dante Alighieri. He appears within the tale as an alternative expert upon whom the Visconti could allegedly call. Dante was indeed connected to the northern Italian aristocracy – dependent upon them for his livelihood – and we know from other sources that he had knowledge of learned magic; but there is no direct evidence that he had any connection to magical plots against the papacy. Where Dante really matters is in his own writing, perhaps most famously *The Inferno*, a vision of Hell that also commented on the society and politics of his time. The key thing about the poet was that he wrote, proudly, in Italian. He was not the first medieval writer to do such a thing, but he was perhaps the first to make a virtue of it, and to claim the ascendancy of the vernacular, as a poetical language, over Latin. And this made him famous, sufficiently famous that he could be invoked by Galeazzo as a credible, albeit veiled, threat to Bartolomeo.

This was a world in motion, some of its essential elements changing in this very moment. Thus, if one scratches the surface of 'the medieval' something more complex appears. In introducing the study of medieval history, my first task has been to demonstrate that things are not quite as they initially seem. Yes, it was an age when religion loomed much larger than in many modern European countries. Yes, it contained knights and ladies and monks and saints and inquisitors and all the other inhabitants of a thousand lurid historical novels. But it was neither simple nor unchanging. It was not even 'one' thing, in part because when studying the middle ages one may be engaged with more than a thousand years of history and thousands of square miles of geography. But also because if one asked John XXII and Dante Alighieri about the nature of papal power, one would receive two radically different answers. That is, to put the point more broadly, every element of 'medievalness' is situated within a certain perspective, differing between different times, places and people, rather than one universal and univocal feature of the period.

Medievalisms and Historiographies

Over a couple of decades at the end of the seventeenth century, a classical scholar at the University of Halle in Germany, Christopher Cellarius (1638–1707), published a book under the title *Universal History Divided into an Ancient, Medieval and New Period*. Cellarius was far from the first person to subdivide western history into three periods: in his self-conscious links back to a classical tradition, the Italian poet Petrarch (1304–74) had inferred a difference – a darkness – about the period intervening between his own time and the antique past. The lawyer and classicist Pierre Pithou (1539–96) had talked of 'un moyen age', and the antiquarian William Camden (1551–1625) similarly of 'a middle time'. The passing notion of a 'middle age' was not new, but what Cellarius did was to build a complete framework for historical time around the concept. And his book was a textbook, imparted as foundational knowledge. Then and ever after, western historians have talked of 'antiquity', 'the middle ages' and 'modernity'.

The important thing to note here is that, from the first moments of its inception, 'medieval' has been a term of denigration. For Petrarch and later humanists, for the antiquarians, for Pithou and for later Enlightenment philosophers, what mattered was the classical past, and the ways in which it informed and was renewed by the 'modern' world around them. Both the ancient 'then' and the contemporary 'now' were thrown into stark relief by the darkness in between: a darkness of ignorance, decay, chaos, confusion, anarchy and unreason. As the early modern period 'rediscovered' (largely via the very middle ages it disparaged) texts and artefacts from the Greek and Roman past, using them as models for its own cultural productions, the middle ages came to stand for a gross barbarity of style and language. Medieval historians were disparaged for their failure to conform to classical modes of rhetoric. Its art was seen as hopelessly unsophisticated, its literature as clumsy, its music similarly lacking. The judgements passed on medieval politics were of a similar, almost aesthetic, vein. As the economist Anne-Robert-Jacques Turgot (1727–81) characterized the period:

> The kings without any authority, the nobles without any constraint, the peoples enslaved, the countryside covered with fortresses and ceaselessly ravaged, wars kindled between city and city, village and village . . . all commerce and all communications cut off . . . the grossest ignorance extending over all nations and all occupations! An unhappy picture – but one which was only too true of Europe for several centuries.[4]

As the last century of study has amply demonstrated, Turgot's caricature of the middle ages is grossly distorted. But its spirit continues to reside: we, no less than Enlightenment *philosophes*, tend to look down as we look back, feeling at a gut level that something from the middle ages must be basic, crude and probably nasty. They believed the earth was flat, didn't they? (No, that's a later myth.) They burnt witches, didn't they? (Not very often, that was mostly in the seventeenth century.) They were all ignorant, weren't they? (No, there is substantial intellectual culture visible in Carolingian times, there were universities across Europe from the thirteenth century, and the beginnings of experimental science, among other things.) They never left home, hardly knew the world around them, right? (No, there were trade networks connecting Scandinavia, central Europe, the Middle East and North Africa.) But, surely, they behaved barbarically: constant local violence, waging wars against people they didn't like, torturing people, executing criminals? (And none of this happens today?)

This initial, vast accretion of grime is the first veil that must be removed in order to do medieval history seriously. Put aside preconceptions about the period: some may have elements of truth to them, but they must be treated as a matter for investigation, rather than a foundation. The middle ages were what they were – the many things they were – rather than only the summed 'failures' of future ages' expectations. The medieval was not simply the opposite of what is deemed 'modern'; it was something much more complex, and, as we will see, something still interwoven with how we are today.

The second veil to be penetrated is bestowed by the politics of medievalism. The middle ages have frequently been an object of ideological struggle, even when being disavowed. Thus, for those fifteenth- and sixteenth-century Italian humanists who condemned the preceding centuries to 'darkness', a major consideration was the desire to deny any continuity between the old Roman Empire and the medieval Holy Roman Empire – because of the legitimacy this would confer on the existing Holy Roman Emperor. For the Enlightenment *philosophes*, a major factor in denigrating the middle ages was its apparent religiosity, in thrall to the command of the Catholic Church: something against which the defenders of Reason, in the eighteenth century, continued to struggle. The nineteenth century brought, in several European countries, a more positive attitude towards the medieval: France, for example, fell in love once again with chivalry, while Germany looked back to a powerful combination of law and empire, and England glowed with quiet pride over its long history of parliamentary constitutionalism. But these reinventions of the medieval were also political, informed particularly by different strands of Romantic nationalism. Because of events in the mid-twentieth century, we tend to see this as most poisonous in Germany, and certainly German historiography in the nineteenth century sought the roots of its *Volksgeist* in the medieval past, and looked back to the 'glory days' of the Empire. But it was a weakness to which every European country was prone, and while the medievalisms that it fostered varied according to nationality, they shared the tendency to romanticize, mythologize and simplify the medieval past.

This is not to say that this reappropriation is all that the nineteenth century gave us. General histories of modern historiography tend to talk of a 'revolution' in historical method in the nineteenth century, associated particularly with Leopold von Ranke (1795–1886) and German historiography more broadly. While there are reasons for being suspicious of some of the claims made by and about Ranke with regard to how revolutionary the use of primary archival sources actually was,[5] it is definitely the case that the foundations of modern, academic history were laid by Germany in the nineteenth century, and that a focus on archives and source analysis was a primary part of this. Some version of Rankean historiography informed the creation of academic history teaching, and subsequently postgraduate training, in France, Italy, England, the US and elsewhere. As various writers have shown, it was rare that the adopters of von Ranke's ideas understood them quite in the way he intended: they tended to reify the notion of a 'scientific method' in an unwarranted fashion, and failed to see the abstract, spiritual element in Ranke's call for the historian *wie es eigentlich gewesen ist* ('only to show what actually [or, more accurately, 'essentially'] happened').[6] Moreover, while Ranke had broad interests in the Renaissance and Reformation periods, his followers tended to restrict their focus to high political history, based on study of governmental archives, which meant that pre-existing interests in social and cultural history were sidelined as rather 'amateurish' pursuits.

In England, in particular, the professionalization of history over the course of the late nineteenth and early twentieth centuries was played out in the study of the middle ages. This partly followed the German example – in both countries, it had been medieval records that formed the basis for the great series of edited sources, the *Monumenta Germaniae Historica* (begun 1826) and the Rolls Series (begun 1857) – but also reflected both an English pride in its long constitutional history, and an English abhorrence for current political argument. The middle ages, it was felt, was a suitably distant period for university study, unlikely to lead to unseemly debate and dissension among modern undergraduates. For Oxford and Cambridge, in the pre-war years, medieval history was political precisely by dint of being apolitical: no current religious debates or party political issues to cause upset, and hence a suitable arena of study for the developing minds of the Empire's future administrators. A succession of Grand Old Men of English medievalism is associated with both universities in the late nineteenth century, but none of them is now read for any present insight. They excluded from their middle ages anything that unbalanced the smooth progress of the ship of state; assumed rather than analysed the case for English 'exceptionalism', thus furthering England's tendency to look inward rather than outward; and a thick blanket of social and political complacency slumps suffocatingly over their prose. The interesting research and teaching were being done in London and Manchester, by figures such as A. F. Pollard and T. F. Tout; and the most exciting work was by a scholar of law, rather than history, F. W. Maitland.[7] Maitland is still worth reading today, for while later research has corrected some of the details of his work, his sensitive understanding of law's structural relationship to society continues to inspire.[8]

The next 'revolution' in historiography also had a strong medieval element, this time in France. Lucien Febvre and Marc Bloch, two graduates of the École normale supérieure, had a new vision for what history could become. The perspectives associated with the pair have become known by the title of the journal they founded: the *Annales*. Febvre's work concerned the early modern period, but Bloch was a medievalist. They wanted to broaden the horizon of historiography, free it from the pursuit of factual political narrative and explore instead the fields of geography, society, culture, even the psyche. Strongly influenced by sociology and anthropology, Bloch's vision of the middle ages was complex and panoramic. His two-volume *Feudal Society* attempted to construct an analysis of the period, changing over time, that emphasized structural connections that ran vertically through all of society. Scholarship has moved on here in various ways, and (as we shall see in Chapter 4) arguments about the nature of feudalism have altered considerably since Bloch's day; but his attempt at writing a complete history, sensitive to all parts of the medieval landscape, remains a solitary beacon. Bloch's other great legacy was his book on historiography, *Apologie pour l'histoire, ou Métier d'historien* (published posthumously and translated into English as *The Historian's Craft*). Despite being unfinished – Bloch, a member of the French resistance, was still writing it when murdered by the Gestapo in 1944 – it continues to provide a brilliant introduction to doing history.[9]

The *Annales* mode of historiography continued strongly, never following a strict orthodoxy, but, rather, a broad perspective and set of complementary inclinations. Georges Duby and Jacques Le Goff developed Bloch's legacy, the former pursuing in particular the important shifts in socioeconomic structures, the latter more interested in the cultural *mentalité* of the period. For all the French medievalists, Marxism provided a useful set of intellectual tools, and in the case of Duby in particular, encouraged the careful study of economic relations in understanding social structures. There had been earlier Marxist works of medieval history – Gaetano Salvemini had published a book on late thirteenth-century Florence in 1899 that considered its society in terms of class structures – but it was the *Annales* that brought theory sustainedly to bear on the period.

This is not to say that Bloch, Duby, Le Goff and others were all Marxists in a personal sense; indeed, in a broader perspective, the *Annales* group were distanced from the more explicitly Marxist traditions. It was, rather, that the French educational system, then as today, saw the insights of Marxism as part of the intellectual landscape. In the latter half of the twentieth century, there were some medievalists writing within Communist societies: a number of East German scholars, and the Russian Aron Gurevich. The work of the former was deleteriously affected by their political context, restricted to following the Party line on topics such as medieval heresy (where one had to parrot the perspectives of Friedrich Engels's brief comments in his *Peasant War in Germany*) and the reflexive conflation of ecclesiastical and secular powers. Gurevich, inspired by the *Annales* tradition, but with a helpfully critical distance from it, is a very different case. His work was hampered by his relative lack of access to archival source materials, but this handicap inspired deep reflection on medieval society and culture, with a particular pursuit of the cultural fissures between medieval social classes. Marxism also provided a particular boost for historiography in England: the influential Historians' Group of the British Communist Party, which existed from 1946 to 1956, established a new historiographical tradition not dissimilar to that of the *Annales*, but with a more clearly political intent. Its medieval element resided particularly with Rodney Hilton, whose work pursued the theme of class conflict in medieval English society.[10] *Past and Present*, the journal founded by the Historians' Group, though itself now no longer wedded to Marxism, continues to provide a strong platform for medieval enquiry, among other periods.

Work in America has in part followed European tides – as in other countries, many American medievalists of the early twentieth century did their training in Germany, and brought Rankean models of historiographical pedagogy back to their own universities – but has also developed its own foci and interests.[11] The particularly American revolution in historiography, the 'New History' associated with Carl Becker and Charles Beard post-World War I, was notably unpopular with medievalists, who remained staunch defenders of 'scientific objectivity' against this perceived relativism. The biggest influence on medieval history in the first half of the twentieth century was an underlying commitment to modernizing 'Progressive' politics, associated with President Woodrow Wilson. Indeed, one of the formative figures in medieval studies, Charles Homer Haskins (1870–1937), was a friend and adviser to Wilson; and through Haskins's student Joseph Strayer, and Strayer's many graduate students, one can trace a continued line of interest in the growth of the medieval state, the modernizing elements within medieval society, and so forth.

Overall, the shifts within medieval history in the twentieth century largely followed broader currents in historiography. The Rankean period of professionalization focused its energy particularly on studies of high politics, with accompanying interests in the history of the law and the development of national constitutions. Over time, historiography came to admit medieval society and economics as legitimate areas that expanded the possibilities of the discipline; religion, for example, could be analysed as a sociocultural phenomenon rather than simply ecclesiastical governance. Women became a topic for sustained study particularly in the 1970s (though pioneering work in this area dates back to the late nineteenth century and early twentieth century, for example by the economic historian Eileen Power), and the presence and treatment of minorities – Jews, lepers, heretics, homosexuals, slaves and 'Saracens' – in the 1980s (though excellent work on Jews and heretics had already appeared some decades earlier), and in both cases American scholars largely led the way. New philosophies of history, often rather loosely and not very helpfully termed 'postmodernism', have occasioned medievalist engagement, most explicitly (both pro- and anti-) in the US and France.[12] The shifts had many causes, some stretching out into academia far beyond the particular field of medievalism, but all were facilitated by the entry into academe of people from more diverse backgrounds than the overwhelmingly white, male and strongly patrician founding fathers of the early twentieth century.

Developments in historiography, of which the preceding paragraphs offer but a crude summary, did not of course end in the 1980s, and the movement from politics to culture has not been a linear path; indeed, a particular move in recent times has been the looping back of culture to politics. To this, and other topics of recent interest, we shall turn in later chapters. Nor does the preceding sketch mention a host of individually important figures for the development of the discipline, such as the nineteenth-century American scholar of inquisition Henry Charles Lea, or the Oxford don Richard Southern whose mixture of intellectual and cultural history inspired a generation, or many other more recent figures such as Caroline Walker Bynum, Barbara Hanawalt, Janet Nelson or Miri Rubin (to correct the earlier gender imbalance somewhat).

But, given the constraints of brevity, what should we take from the brief introduction above? I want to suggest that there are four problems of which any student of medieval history should be aware, and one overarching issue. The last I shall turn to at the end of this chapter; let us look first at the problems.

The Politics of Framing

First is the lurking presence of nationalism, that key element in nineteenth-century Romantic ideology. The degree to which issues of race and nation informed the creation of modern medieval studies cannot be underplayed. Ranke and his disciples searched for the 'essence' in history, and that essence was quickly identified first with a *Volksgeist* (a 'spirit of the people') and then with a national and racial destiny. The medieval past provided an essential ballast to national unity and strength: when the Prussian army defeated Napoleon III in 1870, Georges Monod (founder of the *Revue Historique* and an historian of early medieval France) ascribed the German victory to the strength of national unity fostered by that country's historians, and shortly thereafter French schools introduced classes in 'civic instruction' based on the study of French history.[13] Ernst Kantorowicz's populist biography of Frederick II, the thirteenth-century Holy Roman Emperor, was a great success in his native Germany in the 1930s, and this was due at least in part to the attraction of the past 'German' empire to the audience of that time, and possibly also the vision of a strong, charismatic leader for the German people, at just the moment that Adolf Hitler was elected as Chancellor (though Kantorowicz himself later abhorred this connection, and indeed fled Nazi Germany).[14] This is not to suggest that medieval study, past or present, is fatally tainted by the later horrors of Nazi Europe; most historiography of the nineteenth century was affected by nationalism to some extent or other, and one should not abandon all elements of nineteenth-century Romanticism or philosophy because of later uses to which it was put.[15] But medieval history did play a particular role here, having been at the vanguard of historiographic developments over the period 1830–1930, and the link must be recognized, for its legacy if nothing else. As noted also in the final chapter of this book, in recent times various neo-Nazi groups have wished to appropriate elements of these foundational narratives, turning a highly distorted version of a uniformly 'white', Christian middle ages into an ideological weapon.

A less fraught version of that legacy, the second problem, is the extent to which study of the middle ages continues to be framed, often unwittingly, by the attitudes, interests and concepts of the nineteenth century. First among those is the very idea of 'nation': we live in modern nation-states, our mother tongues tend to lead us to identify ourselves along national lines, and we correspondingly find it convenient to think of the world, both past and present, in terms of national boundaries. Indeed, I talked of 'Italy' in the first paragraph of this book, and mentioned 'France' and 'Spain' soon thereafter; in each case, this was to help the reader locate the action geographically. But these modern geographies fit awkwardly with changing medieval realities. There was no unified 'Italy' at any point after the late sixth century – rather, the Italian peninsula was continually carved up in different ways between the Holy Roman Emperor, the papacy and whichever monarch held the throne of Sicily (this being the very context for the Visconti plot against John XXII). The strongest allegiances felt by people in what we now call northern Italy were frequently to a particular city-state – Milan, Venice, Florence – and not to a nation. Spain similarly did not exist in its modern form: for centuries, much of the Iberian Peninsula was under Muslim rule, and the Christian portions (expanding south in spasms of conquest, particularly in the eleventh, early thirteenth and fifteenth centuries) were divided into several separate kingdoms until the end of the middle ages. France is perhaps a slightly clearer entity, but the French kingdom in the period I mentioned – the early thirteenth century – had expanded far beyond the Île-de-France (into Flanders and lands previously held by kings of England) only in the preceding two decades, with Aquitaine still in English hands, Burgundy essentially separate, and Languedoc only coming into French possession in 1271. Even England, with arguably the most centralized kingship of any country from soon after the Norman Conquest, could be seen as a rather loose entity, with uncertain borders to the north and west, and a questionable sense of relationship to its holdings in what is now France. None of these labels – English, French, Spanish, Italian, German – is terribly helpful when applied to the early middle ages; and can, indeed, be deeply misleading even for later periods.

So medievalists now need to think about nations critically rather than unproblematically celebrating them. Other hand-me-down concepts from the founders of medieval history have also been questioned in recent years: the coherence, in their contemporary settings, of different 'bodies' of law (Roman law and canon law in particular); the sense in which the Catholic Church was a singular, unitary entity; and the notion that there is a kind of 'hierarchy' of sources, moving initially from the official histories to governmental archives, and thence to 'lesser' materials. Anglophone medievalism has had a particular trait of Victorian (and later) scholarship to deal with: its tendency to ignore or even suppress 'vulgar' elements of the past that it found unseemly or which did not fit with its picture of the period. Thus, for example, Eileen Power's 1928 translation of the late fourteenth-century advice manual *Le Menagier de Paris* omits most discussion of sexual sins, out of deference for its modern readership.[16] And all histories of emergent 'modernity', while frequently focused on 'national' wars and struggles, have tended to homogenize and homeostatize the society of the middle ages, emphasizing its simplicity and organic changelessness rather than seeking out elements of social conflict, cultural friction or gendered struggle.

Of course, the last half-century or so of historiography has revised opinions in many of these areas. But traces of them still lurk, at their most distorting when not immediately obvious to modern practitioners. All forms of academic study periodically grapple with the conditions of their existence, and the legacies of their founders; such wrestling is informative, useful, necessary, but should not be the whole story or lead us into analytical paralysis. Nonetheless, the second caveat stands: remember where we came from.

The third problem is of a different order. The differences in national historiographical trends sketched above (focused particularly on Germany, France, the UK and the US) have persisted. The historical study of the middle ages is conducted, in each of those places today, under differing conditions, within differing traditions, with differing expectations, and to some degree in pursuit of different ends. How history itself is periodized can vary from country to country and area to area: Italian historiography, for example, tends to relinquish 'medieval' for 'Renaissance' at some point in the fourteenth century, while some strands of French research treat '*l'ancien régime*' as an entity that stretched from medieval times up to the Revolution without a significant break.

In broad terms, the academic pursuits of each country have tended to have their individual timbre. France has long delighted in intellectual superstructures, more willing to sacrifice detail to the larger analysis, and examine *la longue durée* in an attempt to divine the structural essence of a period. French efforts, in this as in much else, often disgruntle the English, who are more frequently empiricist in method, focused on the particular and the local, insistent on the importance of details and exceptions. Germany is perhaps also more wedded to large-scale intellectual tools than England, but tools rather different from France's: more usually a key defining concept such as 'symbolic communication', which is used heuristically to provoke specific questions in a methodical way. The US – its academic community larger by far – has taken elements from all these traditions, but has also perhaps tended to fetishize the (admittedly important) technical skills that medievalists deploy when studying original manuscripts, possibly paradoxically because of American scholars' geographical dislocation from the archives they study. At the same time, that distance has also perhaps encouraged more structurally comparative and theoretical work in the US.

Also important are the different material conditions under which scholars work. Germany and France have extremely centralized systems of training and subsequent recruitment, and one outcome from this is a very strong patronage system (as is also the case in Italy), which tends to lead research either into patrilineal currents of development, or else spasms of Oedipal rebellion. Elements of this are present elsewhere, but much less institutionally inevitable. Funding for study in Germany largely operates through the collaborative model of the sciences, building 'research institutes' focused on a particular issue over a period of years, whereas, until recently at any rate, funding and research in the US and UK have been very individualistic. In both the US and, particularly, the UK, early career scholars live under a 'publish or perish' regime, which means that first books tend to come swiftly and noisily, as academics try to secure their first job or tenure. Another difference is the location and nature of archives. England has long had both a centralized national archive, and (from the mid-twentieth century) local record offices; in recent decades these, like other important libraries such as the British Library and the Warburg Institute, have had a very 'customer-orientated' policy of access. France, while possessing several national libraries and many local archives, is rather more bureaucratically bound; negotiating access to a manuscript in the Bibliothèque nationale in Paris, for example, involves the complex transference of three separate pieces of plastic card and several slips of paper between the researcher and the archivist. This does have an effect on the speed of the research that can be undertaken, if nothing else. Both Germany's and Italy's archives have always been regional, which thus affects the shape of the scholarship done there: very few Italian medievalists work comparatively across different city-states, for example.

None of these national differences is absolute or insuperable, and the entrance of further players into the game – Spain, Poland, Japan, Hungary – helps to foster better communication across borders. All countries complain that their scholarship is insufficiently read abroad: at a conference I attended when first writing this book, I had identical conversations along this line with two distinguished scholars, one English and one French, each bewailing the tendency of the other's country to ignore their compatriots' work. But conversations do happen, books get read, translated, discussed, ideas pass across borders, are reshaped in the process, then handed back to their progenitors in new forms. Medieval history is an international conversation, which is part of its pleasure; nonetheless, any student of the period must be aware of its national inflections.

The fourth and final problem is whether there was a 'middle ages' at all. As we have seen above, the notion of a different (and lesser) period separating the classical past from the 'modern' age was the invention of Renaissance humanists, and became a solidified periodization in the seventeenth century. We have got into the habit, over the course of the last few centuries, of talking about 'medieval' this and 'the middle ages' that. For those of us working in academe, 'medievalist' often tends to be a source of professional identity (which, if nothing else, excuses us from knowing about things outside our period). But none of this is an essence drawn from the past. We could attempt to periodize differently – or not at all. The notional boundaries between 'late antiquity', 'medieval' and 'early modern' (or indeed 'Renaissance') are all deeply problematic, inevitably Eurocentric, and can obscure as much as they reveal. At the earlier end, for example, historians have increasingly seen continuities between some Roman structures and practices and later 'barbarian' principalities; at the later juncture, there has been great debate over the degree to which intellectual, cultural and political developments of the Renaissance were prefigured in twelfth- and thirteenth-century Europe.

However, most who work on some aspect of the period 500–1500 do tend to feel, whether consciously or not, that it has some features that distinguish it (or parts of it – we usually specialize within that 1,000-year span) from earlier or particularly later eras. These are predominantly European features, though not exclusively so. We are looking at past times, from after the end of the Roman Empire, but before the expansion of western colonialism. In almost all places, the basis of the economy was agricultural, resting on exploiting labour surplus from a large mass of more or less subservient peasants. Communication across regions was relatively slow, and could not be relied upon to be uniform in content or reception; power structures tended to rely heavily upon intra-personal relations, and where bureaucracies developed they were fragile in comparison to later times. The human experiences that left their marks on the written archive were always but a small fraction of the totality that once existed. None of this absolutely distinguishes 'the middle ages' from other periods, nor do these features pertain in all times and places;

but they indicate some shared centre of expectation for those studying it. A crude but perhaps useful way of reflecting on this is to think critically about the alterity, the 'otherness', of the middle ages – as I suggested at the beginning of this chapter. We may have certain expectations of medieval 'otherness' drawn from popular culture; these can be put to one side, albeit perhaps with some effort. But there is a more profound question that historians must confront: were medieval people like us, or were they fundamentally different? Or, to put it with greater nuance, at what points must one entertain the possibility of fundamental difference between then and now, and at what points might one consider essential continuities? This is a theme to which we shall return throughout the book.

While some historians do attempt to chase themes over a very *longue durée* – pursuing a history of death from antiquity to modernity, for example – the majority specialize in particular periods, and the depth of knowledge that this facilitates is undoubtedly useful. But it should perhaps be best remembered as a professional and intellectual choice rather than something that the past somehow foists upon us; and, as I will suggest later in this book, medievalists must also try to think about how they might speak beyond their own period, to join in even larger conversations than those they hold between themselves. Because framing the middle ages – placing it into some meaningful context or narrative – has always been and will always be a political act, as well as an historiographical one. This is the overarching issue mentioned above, and it informs, wittingly or unwittingly, all that we do as medieval historians. 'The middle ages', however they are understood, have always been part of a wider argument, even if only tacitly, about 'progress', 'government', 'human nature', 'civilization', and so forth. They currently play a particular role in arguments about the perceived 'clash of civilizations' between West and East, in the denunciation by some commentators of particular Islamic practices as 'medieval', in the use of the term 'crusade' by both an American president and anti-western Islamic radicals, and in the very sense in which 'West' is assumed to be geopolitically opposed to 'East'. Doing history is political, and doing medieval history no less so than other, more recent, periods.

2
Tracing the Middle Ages

Polyphony or Cacophony?

The rising began on 30 May 1381 at Brentwood in Essex, as arrows were fired at some justices of the peace. They were attempting to collect the third poll tax that, under the leadership of John of Gaunt, had been levied by the young Richard II's government. The peasantry of England was no longer willing to accede to such demands however, and within a few days the country was in rebellion, with commoners from Kent and Essex marching on London, and separate risings occurring in East Anglia, Yorkshire and elsewhere. In London, the rebels destroyed buildings and property, burnt documents and beheaded several royal officials, including the archbishop of Canterbury. Under the leadership of Wat Tyler, they demanded an end to serfdom and lordship, the disendowment of the Church, and that the lands of lords and bishops be divided between the common folk. Tyler, however, was killed at Smithfield for insulting behaviour in the king's presence, and Richard II managed to convince the mob to leave the city peacefully. Thereafter many were hanged and fined; 'and thus ended this evil war'.[1]

So, at any rate, one important source tells it. Another fails to mention the tax collectors at the beginning of events, and depicts instead an organized and armed bid for liberty arising in Essex, copied then in Kent, and initially directed against lawyers and ancient customs. A third source does talk about tax collectors, but suggests that they had been harassing women in the villages, this being the original cause of dissension. The Peasants' Revolt of 1381 – or the English Rising, or Rebellion, or Revolution, or Insurrection, depending on how one wishes to label and thus interpret it – is one of the most famous events in medieval English history. It has been a topic of investigation and debate ever since it occurred. But that does not mean that all is known or settled about the matter; indeed, quite radical reappraisals of the events of 1381 have been presented in recent years. In part this is because of the different conceptual tools that have inspired each generation of historians (a topic to be discussed in the next chapter). But a large measure of what permits historians to argue and reinterpret is the nature of the evidence. The surviving textual traces for 1381 are rich and copious. They do not, however, cover every possible detail, they agree on neither all specifics nor generalities and they do not speak with one voice. The evidence is therefore not simply something one reads but something one must work with – in order to find different ways of interpreting, viewing and understanding.

What materials remain extant for 1381? The three sources mentioned above were all chronicle accounts, specifically the *Anonimalle Chronicle*, Thomas Walsingham's *Chronica Maiora* and Henry Knighton's *Chronicon*. Late fourteenth-century England was a particularly rich period for chronicle writing, and a variety of other accounts survive in addition to these three. But these narrative sources are not the only things available. The suppression of the revolt generated quite a large amount of documentary evidence in the form of various regional inquiries, where local jurors made presentments about specific deeds committed by their neighbours during the uprising. Various trial records from the royal courts also survive, detailing the charges and sentences for particular individuals. Other government documents exist: records of Parliament's decisions before and after the revolt, orders given by the king for the suppression of the rising, royal letters of pardon to particular rebels, petitions to the king from other areas affected by the rising, and records relating to the poll tax itself. Transcribed within two of the chronicle accounts are six 'rebel letters', fascinating but frustratingly opaque documents that appear to record rather general or coded rallying cries circulated among the rebels, possibly originally in the form of broadsides (small documents posted up publicly, on church doors for example). The revolt left its mark in other literary places too, from sermons delivered in its aftermath, to brief verses on its suppression, to strands within lengthy poems such as Geoffrey Chaucer's *Canterbury Tales*, John Gower's *Vox Clamantis* and William Langland's *Piers Plowman*, the latter apparently revised in the aftermath of the revolt lest its call for social and spiritual reform be seen as too sympathetic to the rising.

It is immediately apparent, from this brief list, that to write a history of 1381 involves more than reading the narrative accounts and repeating what they say. For a start, the various sources do not agree. At points, they sing together in complex polyphony, but on some issues (the composition and aims of the rebels, for example) they produce a discordant clamour. An attempt to synthesize one version of events from all the evidence inevitably means that one must make selections and take interpretative decisions – silence some voices, in other words. For a long time, the main chronicles were given precedence, and this led historians in certain directions, in particular a tendency to see the rebels through those chroniclers' eyes, as largely uncoordinated scum, drawn from the bottom ranks of society, wild and vicious and ignorant. But research using a different set of sources, the trial records generated in the aftermath of the revolt, has produced a rather different picture. A large proportion of the rebels were from the upper end of village society, the kind of people who held local offices, such as bailiffs and jurors. This suggests that their actions were of a rather different order and nature.[2] Moreover, the history one writes is affected not only by what sources one uses but how one uses them. In order to see the pattern of social composition of the revolt, the trial documents needed to be subjected to statistical analysis, calculating the numbers of people mentioned by their varied socioeconomic levels. To see how Langland revised his poem in the aftermath of revolt, some very careful comparative work on various surviving manuscripts needed to be done.

Even the best-known chronicle sources have been opened

up to new perspectives in recent analysis, by reading them 'against the grain': that is, by looking for confusions, contradictions, elisions or other indications of tension within the texts that might allow one to see what the author was not saying, or saying between the lines, whether deliberately or subconsciously.

But in discussing interpretative techniques, we are getting ahead of ourselves. Let us begin with a more basic question: where do we find medieval sources?

Editions and Archives

The simple response is, we find the sources in libraries and archives (and, increasingly, online). However, this hides further complexities. As nascent historians, we usually first meet primary sources in modern printed editions (and in translation), and indeed most historians continue to use at least some printed sources in their later research. They are invaluable, partly because of their relative ease of availability and also because part of the hard initial work has often already been done by the editor: creating an index, explaining the immediate context, ascertaining the author, and so forth. One of the main foundations of modern, academic history was the creation of grand, collaborative series of printed documents: Ludovico Muratori's *Rerum Italicarum Scriptores* begun in the early eighteenth century, the German *Monumenta Germaniae Historica*, the English Rolls Series, and Abbé Migne's *Patrologia Latina* to mention the most extensive four. Without these efforts, modern historiography would look very different.

But such series are not without their problems. There is the question of editorial selection, informed by certain historiographical and nationalist (or, in Migne's case, religious) assumptions. In every case, the series present a preponderance of chronicle or other narratives, establishing a 'canon' of important works. Certain kinds of document, such as the copious records of local manors, were rarely seen as sufficiently important to be edited, because they did not concern the deeds of 'great men', and were not of 'national' importance (although the various local record series, published particularly in England, have gone some way to remedying this bias). The classic print editions thus tended to direct attention towards certain areas, and occlude others: the role of women in medieval society, for example, is hardly visible in narrative sources like monastic chronicles, but has become much more so when other forms of documentation such as religious writings or local records are examined. Second, a print edition fixes in aspic what were originally more fluid texts. For example, the original editors of the Rolls Series, dealing with a series of manuscript chronicles from the abbey of St Albans, published them under four separate titles, assuming no overall author. Later work argued that all four were in fact different stages in the development of one chronicle written by Thomas Walsingham; or, perhaps, a major chronicle (*Chronica Maiora*) and a shorter version. More recently, however, a close examination of original manuscripts, rather than the print editions, has suggested a yet more complex picture of multi-authored compositions in various stages of production.[3] Conversely, the creation of an edited text often demands that one condense the slightly differing contents of several manuscript versions into one 'authoritative' amalgam. The means by which one does this, and the possibilities of demonstrating divergent readings, continue to be explored and debated by modern editors.[4] Nineteenth-century editions are often now seen to be flawed in this respect, either dependent upon a notion of textual 'purity' that modern scholars no longer find useful or convincing, or (particularly in the case of the *Patrologia Latina*) prey to poor and opportunistic editorial decisions.[5] Later historians have been as interested in manuscript variations as in the 'original' texts themselves (if an 'original' can actually be located): that Langland altered his poem is at least as important a fact as determining either the first or final versions of *Piers Plowman*, and changes that Walsingham made in later recensions of his chronicle tell us as much about the political vicissitudes in late medieval England as the details contained within any one 'best' or 'final' version.

None of this means that historians shun printed editions. They are terribly convenient: a good university library will hold at least some, and national research libraries will likely have the lot. But for in-depth research, historians often want to check the manuscripts of even well-known sources. And, of course, many more things survive in manuscript and document form than have been put into print. For these, one must usually turn to modern archives of medieval documents.

Where records reside today depends in large part on how and why they were originally created and kept. There are a few fantastic finds in unorthodox locations: the American medievalist Robert Brentano discovered some very rich local ecclesiastical records in the bell tower of a small Italian church, and quite a number of important medieval documents have been found used as bindings for later books.[6] Manuscripts deemed precious by later ages – works by famous authors, such as Chaucer or Dante, or beautiful books of hours and illuminated bibles – are often now found where the money to buy them is (or once was): in national libraries, such as the Bibliothèque nationale in Paris, or the Royal Library in Stockholm, in Oxford and Cambridge colleges, or in elite American universities or private research libraries (the Huntington Library in California for instance).

But most run-of-the-mill written sources survive because they were the product of an authority that wished to preserve them for possible future use. The authority with the largest European reach was the papacy, and the Vatican archives contain a wealth of documentation about ecclesiastical government and administration, as well as more spiritual works – although it was difficult for historians to gain access to this until relatively recent times. In France and England in particular, the national archives were largely the product of increased and centralized bureaucracy from the twelfth and thirteenth centuries. The records they contain are thus predominantly the creations of royal government and justice: national tax assessments (such as one in England in 1377, presaging the revolt four years later), courts of royal justice, governmental letters, parliamentary decisions, and so forth. In other countries, such as Italy and Germany, this kind of centralization never happened during the medieval period, and archives continue to be much more dispersed. Cities such as Florence and Orvieto have 'state archives', which contain documents relating to mechanisms of medieval government, but the geographical scope of these is limited to the lands controlled by the particular city-state – admittedly extensive in some cases (such as Venice), but not corresponding to the modern nation.[7]

In addition to the central archives, both England and France also have regional record offices, which tend to hold different kinds of documents: particularly local administrative records (charters of land transactions, the proceedings of manor and leet courts, for example), but often also ecclesiastical documents (parochial visitations, wills, tithe records). In France, even small villages may still have some records going back to the middle ages under the care of the local mayor. As discussed in the previous chapter, the greater availability of these kinds of materials had a considerable impact on the kind of history one could pursue in the second half of the twentieth century. Prior to high-medieval developments in secular bureaucracy, the majority of west European archives were the creation of monasteries, which acted as repositories for not only records of a religious nature, but also charters of land transfers or other important decisions. The nature of record preservation is therefore evidence itself for how particular medieval societies acted: what kinds of information they deemed important, what they thought of as authoritative, how much the written record mattered for future consultation.[8] A fantastically rich archive of Jewish sources from the early middle ages survives because of a practice common to all religions in Egypt of that time: any document that might have written on it the name of God could not be thrown away lest it be desecrated, even if the contents had no practical importance. Such documents were stored in a room known as a Geniza, and in the Cairo Geniza the historian S. D. Goitein discovered hundreds of thousands of pages of material.[9] Documentary sources are sparse for some parts of the world. For sub-Saharan Africa, for example, we are very heavily reliant on narrative sources mostly written by writers based beyond the region, and this may accurately reflect a relative paucity of written records originally created in that time and place. In western Europe, conversely, much more of what was once created has now been lost, principally because some documents were perceived as being of no further use and were discarded, but also because of later events. In France, for example, the aftermath of the Revolution of 1789 saw large-scale destruction of medieval documents and artefacts, as symbols of the *ancien régime* that had been overthrown. In England, during iconoclastic phases of the Reformation, many stained-glass windows, sculptures, paintings, rood screens and even manuscript illuminations were defaced or destroyed. Losses have continued in more recent times, with widespread collateral losses of buildings and archives during the First and Second World Wars, and, for example, more targeted destruction by combatants during the Spanish Civil War.

Using Documents

Knowing what one wants to do (in the sense of knowing what area one wants to investigate) is not always straight-forward, and does not always precede the encounter with the source material. It is possible to bump into an interesting source while searching for something quite different, and it is frequently the case that the sources cannot answer one's initial question, but prompt the reformulation of the inquiry in a new and more productive direction. When first looking for materials, one usually begins with the assistance of vari-ous 'finding-aids' for archival sources, from brief catalogue entries that describe manuscripts, to detailed 'calendars' that summarize, item by item, their contents. Many are printed and, increasingly, some are available electronically, though most local archives will also have handwritten finding-aids, compiled by generations of archivists, only available to those who actually visit. Even then, much is uncatalogued, or poorly catalogued, and, particularly for the later middle ages, it is possible to find material previously missed or little noted.

Having located one's material, there are, of course, a number of questions that any historian asks: what type of document is it, what or who was it for? Who wrote this, under what conditions? When was it written and when was it read? Why was it created? And so on and so forth. But there are some matters that are more particular to medieval documents. The first and most obvious is actually reading the document in the first place. The vast majority of western medieval sources were written in Latin, and often a form of Latin inflected by the vernacular language of the scribe. The style of Latin and, to some degree, the vocabulary used thus vary over time, place and context. Some chronicles and some verbose papal bulls are particularly demanding, because of their ornate style of writing. On the other hand, many types of document are deeply repetitive and draw on a limited lexicon: sessions of a manor court, for example, are not tremendously taxing once one has grasped their particular vocabulary.

So some degree of Latin is usually a *sine qua non* ('that without which one cannot do') for medievalists. Documents do exist in the vernacular, either from regions that were never particularly subject to Latinate culture, such as northern Scandinavia, or those where a high level of lay literacy entered the documentary record at a relatively early stage, such as northern Italy. But the vernacular languages were not identical to their modern equivalents, nor were they regularized across regions: Middle High German would be hard for a modern German national to understand, and Occitan, the romance language spoken and written in southern France, differs considerably from both modern French and medieval northern French. Both Old English and Middle English employ letter forms that have subsequently disappeared, although the latter is often quite comprehensible when read out loud if you know that thorn (þ) is pronounced 'th', and yogh (ȝ) as usually either the 'y' of 'yoghurt' or the 'i' of 'imp'.[10] An historian of medieval England may also want to read Anglo-Norman French, which was used in Arthurian romances, some chronicles and letters, and for late-medieval legal records and parliamentary legislation. Some medievalists are particularly gifted at languages, and have expertise not only in the modern literature of several European countries but a reading knowledge of many medieval vernaculars. For study of the medieval middle East and southern Mediterranean basin (and indeed beyond), knowledge of Arabic is extremely useful, though only a relatively small number of western medievalists have thus far managed to master that script and language, and collaboration with area specialists and with scholars from the region itself may prove a more useful path forward. So most medievalists have abilities focused in particular areas: a knowledge of Latin plus reading knowledge in the medieval form of their native language, for example.

There is also the question of handwriting. Some skill in palaeography is useful: even where handwriting is regular (as is usually the case with documents from earlier centuries) one must decode the system of compressions and elisions that scribes used, as written medieval Latin was somewhat like the kind of abbreviated English used when text messaging first appeared on mobile phones, with various letters and word endings often indicated only by technical marks: 'C U l8r', for 'see you later', for example. While the handwriting in early medieval documents was often fairly regular – because not many people knew how to write, and those who did had been taught in a fairly standardized way – there was often no separation between words and no punctuation. In documents from the later middle ages, while word separation and some punctuation do make an appearance, the orthographic challenge is harder, as the numbers of people who could write – but write idiosyncratically and sometimes in a hurry – increased.

The biggest help in working out what a document, written in an archaic language in squiggly handwriting and missing many letters, actually says, is to know what it's likely to say even before you begin to look at it. Many forms of medieval document are extremely formulaic: knowing how a genre of document works – the order in which it will mention certain things, the phrases that are likely to appear, the basic function of the document – is a major step towards understanding what a specific document means. To turn to a clear, albeit non-European, example, many official Japanese documents from the middle ages are presented in a few basic variations on the same formula, and this formula extends not only to particular words and phrases, but to the orthographic layout of the page. Thus the date will appear in the same place, the addressee similarly and, in some forms of document, the name of the scribe at the end of the text. The opening lines will identify what kind of document it is. So even before attempting to work out the specific information contained in a document, a scholar of medieval Japan is able fairly swiftly to see what kind of document she or he is dealing with, when it was written, to whom and from whom, and therefore what it is likely to be about.[11] European medieval documents are not usually quite as structured on the page, but there are

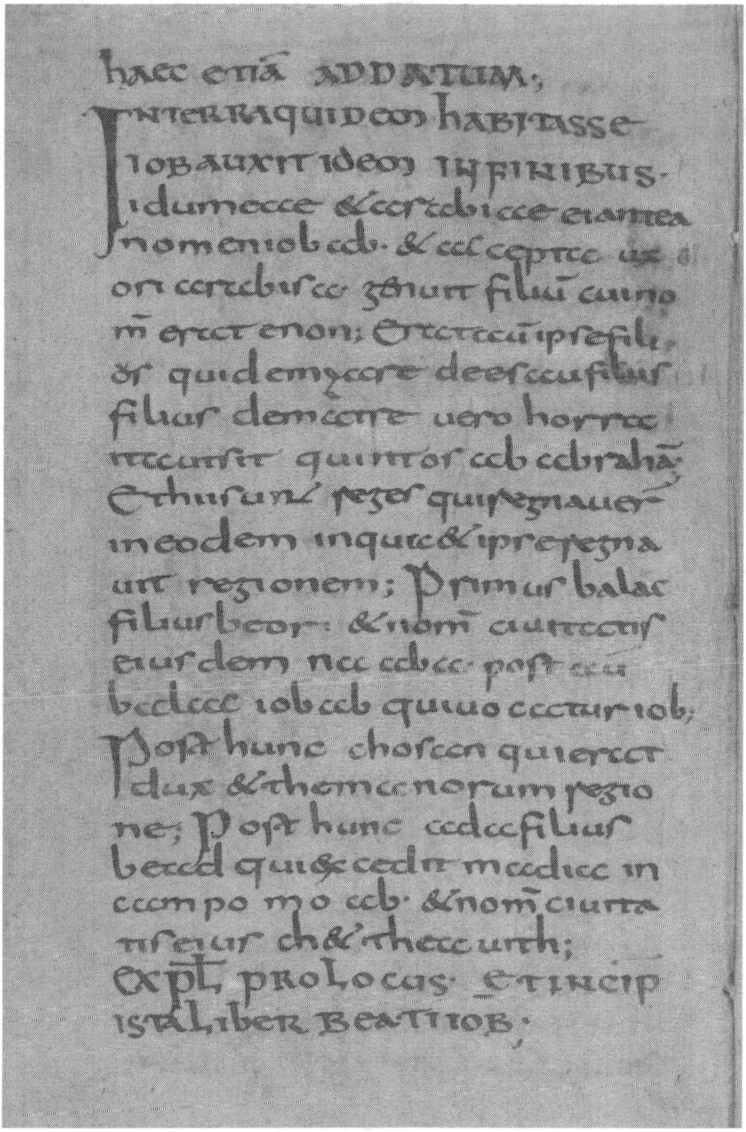

Figure 2.1(a) Early medieval handwriting, from a late eighth-century manuscript of biblical extracts (Cod. Sang. 11, fo. 20, CESG by permission of the Stiftsbibliothek St Gallen)

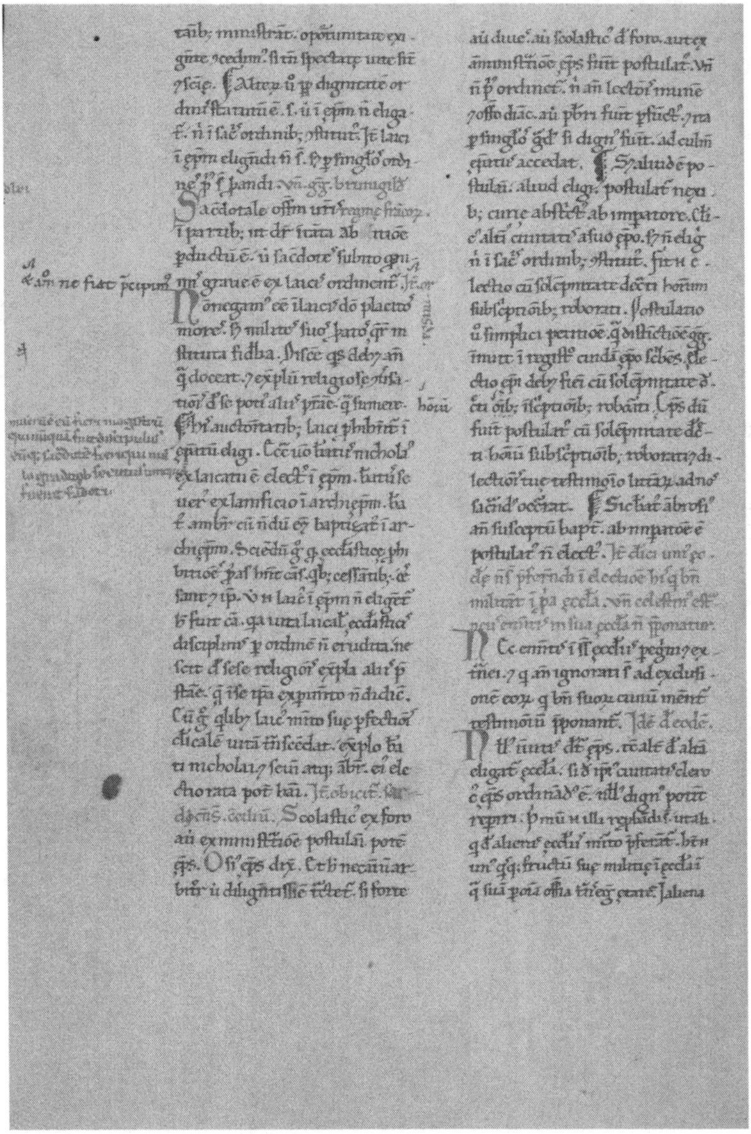

Figure 2.1(b) High medieval handwriting, from a twelfth-century manuscript of canon law (Cod. Sang. 673, fo. 22, CESG by permission of the Stiftsbibliothek St Gallen)

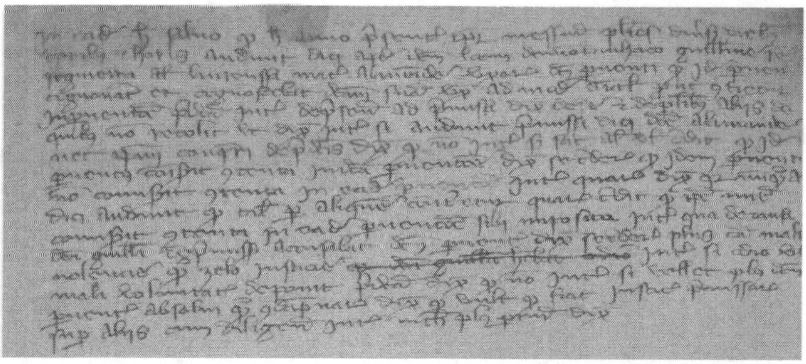

Figure 2.1(c) Later medieval handwriting, in an extract from a civic court record, mid-fourteenth century (Département du Tarn, Archives départementales, 69 EDT FF 18-Bis)

some similarities. Any document beginning *Sciant presentes et futuri* . . . ('All those present and future should know that . . .') is immediately identifiable as a charter, whereas something that, within the first few lines, contains the phrase *In primis lego* [or *commendo*] *animam meam deo* . . . ('Firstly I leave/commend my soul to God') is a late medieval will. In practice, the historian often already knows what kind of document he or she is looking at, because it's what he or she has just requested from the archivist. The formulaic nature of the evidence principally assists with decoding the handwriting and compressions. Thus, someone working on an inquisitorial register and confronted with the terse *I. t. j. d. q.* knows that these should expand to *Item testis juratus dixit quod* . . . ('Item, the sworn witness said that . . .'), because that is what a thousand other entries have similarly said.

The formulaic nature of medieval documents is not only helpful in working out the handwriting, it's also an important element in understanding how the document functions as a whole, and in turn seeing something of how medieval people thought about texts and writing. Take letters, for example. We tend to think of letters as very personal and intimate forms of communication, but this is rarely the case with medieval examples. There were rules of composition, drawn from classical rhetoric, which divided the letter into five parts: a formalized greeting, a quotation designed to put the recipient in a receptive frame of mind, the main narrative or exposition, the request being made by the sender, and the conclusion. Letters were very often public documents, intended for wide circulation beyond the specific recipient, or to set down in quasi-legal fashion a particular decision or instruction for later consultation. Moreover, many letters survive as exemplars of formulaic style, collated in ways foreign to their original compositional contexts.

Another fairly codified text was the sermon, which had notional rules of considerable complexity, and employed a sophisticated chain of ideas about biblical exegesis. This was so, at least, in written form: an essential, but usually unanswerable, question concerning sermons is the relationship between the written text and the presumed oral performance. Occasionally, there are transcripts of actual sermons that may correspond fairly closely to what was said. We have, for example, extensive records in the vernacular for sermons given by Bernardino da Siena in fourteenth-century Tuscany, and the rhetorical power of his very individual performance leaps off the page. At the other extreme, some writers used the form of a sermon as a convenient way of structuring a text, without any intention that it actually be preached. Adam of Dryburgh makes this explicit in his work on the way of life of the Premonstratensian canons, which, he explains, he wrote in the form of fourteen sermons 'so that the understanding of those reading may be enlightened, and their feelings stirred as if it were a present address'.[12] Sermons often employed moral stories known as *exempla* ('examples'), and collections of these survive in considerable numbers, the assumption being that the preacher would make use of those appropriate to his theme at a particular point in the annual sermon cycle. Many *exempla* were intended to be taken as true stories from authentic contemporary or past sources, but others were drawn from classical literature, and yet more were recognized to be useful inventions. An *exemplum* about impious dancers who were cursed by a priest to dance continuously for a year (the dance continuing even beyond death) appears in a fourteenth-century English devotional manual called *Handlyng Synne* written by Robert Mannyng of Brunne.[13] Tales like this have sometimes been taken as indicative of the grotesque credulity of the period, but a careful reading of the text indicates that Mannyng knew that it was a tall story, and knew that his audience would know. As an *exemplum*, it did not even originate in fourteenth-century England, and therefore how one decides to interpret it in this setting is far from straightforward.

In each of these cases, and others, it is therefore important to understand the form that a medieval text takes, the structure to which it is beholden, and the wider compositional assumptions that lie behind it, about intent, meaning, audience and usage. There are many different genres of textual evidence, and it would take a number of large books to cover all these questions in detail. Nonetheless, as a way into the material, let us look at four particular types of source in greater detail: chronicles, charters, images and legal records. These are not categories of equal size or shape – chronicles are a fairly specific kind of text, while images encompass vast variations of size and type – but they help to illustrate some of the different ways in which sources can be used, and the challenges involved in bringing them to life in our histories.

Chronicles

When we think of the medieval chronicle, popular perception might conjure up the image of a tonsured scribe in a remote monastery, at laborious work on a great manuscript that both recounts and denounces the wayward path of the secular world. This is misleading. There certainly were particular monastic centres of chronicle production, such as the abbey of St Denis, which under Abbot Suger began a series of histories in the service of the French kings, and St Albans, home to Roger Wendover, Matthew Paris, Thomas Walsingham and others. But in fact, chronicles often sprang from places other than the monastery: most notably from cities, for which we have chronicle evidence from quite an early period (such as the Pisan annals of *c*.1119), royal courts (many Carolingian histories written in the ninth century were linked in some way to the court) and cathedral chapters (Anselm of Liège's eleventh-century continuation of the *Deeds of the Bishops of Liège*). Much chronicle writing was in Latin, but some vernacular examples appear by the twelfth century, and developed particularly in France and Italy.

Chronicles were thus produced for different purposes, and for different readers, albeit within a fairly limited set of contexts, usually relating to authority. This is true also of how they were reproduced: various manuscripts survive that compile key works of Frankish historiography, working to build a markedly uniform message of Carolingian triumph and legitimacy.[14] A monastic chronicler, such as Rodolphus Glaber ('Ralph the Bald'), could indeed intend the overarching message of his history writing to be a revelation of God's divine plan. Glaber, writing in the early eleventh century, structured his text around a complex system of fourfold divisions, linking (not just symbolically but at a spiritual level) the four corners of the earth, the four ages of the world, the senses of man (sight and hearing conjoined to reduce the number), the four gospels, the four elements, and so on.[15] Glaber's chronicle was dedicated to the abbot of Cluny, and his immediate audience was clearly monastic; yet politics is present here too, as Glaber first describes various troubling events that marked the turn of the millennium – heretics, volcanoes, the deaths of many nobles – in order to then emphasize the restoration of political stability under 'two most Christian kings', Henry of the Saxons and Robert of the Franks.[16] Dino Compagni, a successful merchant and politician, wrote a chronicle of his home city of Florence in the early fourteenth century. His intended audience would have been citizens of his own class – although in fact, due to the shifting political conflicts of the period in which he wrote, his work had to be concealed from his contemporaries, and was not reproduced at all until the late fifteenth century. Compagni's main concern was precisely the factional strife that beset his city, and his sense of how religion inflected history was rather different from that of Glaber: his account of discord and strife was a warning against the consequences of the sin of backbiting, and the spiritual consequences of enmity. What caused such troubles, according to the medieval medical theory Compagni followed, were the physical traits that produced men's characters, such as their tendency towards inflamed passion.[17]

Chronicles were often direct repositories of certain kinds of power, as kings, princes, popes and bishops ensured that important documents were circulated to chronicle-writing centres in order that they be copied into the narrative, and thus preserved and disseminated. The chronicle written by the twelfth-century English monk William of Newburgh contains within it, to give just three examples, the canons of the Third Lateran Council (1179), an important letter from Pope Lucius III to Henry II concerning Saladin's capture of Jerusalem in 1187, and a set of legal statutes from the kings of England and France establishing financial support for the subsequent Third Crusade (1189–92). And the writing of history was frequently the product of trauma, as both Richard Southern and Gabrielle Spiegel have noted: an attempt by one part of the political landscape to deal with changing events by recounting a reassuring version of the past, and to explain change. For example, the west Frankish chronicler Flodoard of Reims wrote in the wake of the deposition of Charles the Simple in 923; similarly, in the aftermath of the Norman Conquest, twelfth-century England saw a great outpouring of chronicles that sought to find a coherent way to narrate, and hence stabilize, the apparently discontinuous history of the realm. In explaining the past to the present, the chronicle is an innately ideological form, yet, as Gabrielle Spiegel puts it, 'all the while dissimulating its status as ideology under the guise of a mere accounting of "what was"'.[18] That dissimulation is, of course, the precise source of its power. *The Chronicle of San Juan de la Peña* (c.1370), commissioned by Pedro IV of Aragon as an official history of his kingdom, was quickly circulated as such throughout the realm, in Latin, Catalan and Aragonese editions.[19] An official history was, in this context, not simply a pleasing ornament to royal power: it asserted the historic basis of that power, laid the ground for Pedro's claim to ancient rights and privileges in the different states that made up Aragon, and defended those rights against outside challenge. This chronicle is thus a political treatise and tool of power as much as a history – but, garbed as 'the past', its claims for Pedro's dominion were much the greater.

What can historians do with chronicles? Obviously they provide a great deal of factual information, and helpful subjective description. The history of early medieval politics would be exceedingly difficult to write without the surviving narrative histories. Some chronicles also record useful flashes of human detail and passion: a chronicle entry concerning an ecclesiastical synod held in 1234 to discuss the murder of a controversial inquisitor reports that one bishop 'burst out "Master Conrad of Marburg [the inquisitor] deserves to be dug up and burnt just like a heretic!"', a detail that illuminates just how unpopular he had become.[20] More endearingly, the tenth-century chronicler Richer of Saint-Rémi includes a chapter devoted solely to the rather difficult time he had on a journey from Reims to Chartres shortly after Easter in 991CE, writing up in classical heroic prose events that essentially boiled down to his party getting lost, the horses tiring out, his boy servant lying down and refusing to get up, and the fact that it was raining: 'Those who have ever suffered similar misfortunes can judge from their own experiences how great my agitation and anxiety were at that moment.'[21] Well, yes.

Chronicles also provide us with some sense of how medievals understood the very fabric of history: time itself. The writing of history in the medieval West was informed by a classical tradition, but set within a Christian eschatological frame: from a Christian perspective, time both began (at the Creation) and would end (with the Apocalypse). History unfolded itself in a linear fashion between these two points; and yet, just as the Old Testament foreshadowed the New, elements of past and future time could overlay themselves on current events. For the period around the year 1000CE, some chroniclers – most famously Ademar of Chabannes and Ralph Glaber – wrote of events framed by elements of millenarian apocalypticism; something similar is found in Ottoman history writers of the fifteenth century, reckoned as the ninth century in the Islamic Hijiri calendar and by Byzantine calculation as the period immediately preceding the 7000th year of creation (at which point the world was expected to end).[22]

For much these same reasons, historians have always been wary of chronicles: information may be distorted, mistaken, fanciful or deliberately misleading. Chroniclers' use of numbers, when estimating sizes of armies or numbers of deaths for example, are often curiously neat and suspiciously high. Matters of patronage and audience can cause quite large distortions: the anonymous *Life of Edward the Confessor*, completed in 1067, avoids all mention of the Norman Conquest, because the purpose of the work was to honour Edward and his dynasty. Chroniclers' subjective assessments, while enlivening, are of course also partisan. Jean de Joinville's vivid portrait of Louis IX's wisdom and holiness was written in the context of the later (successful) campaign to canonize the French monarch, and these sections of his chronicle reflect none of the contemporary criticism of Louis for unworldliness and overdependence on the mendicant orders.[23]

So, unsurprisingly, we note that chroniclers are not always 'trustworthy', whatever that phrase may mean. But one should not seek to avoid or eradicate bias in the chronicle evidence. There were many elements in the world surrounding the chronicler that might affect how he (or very occasionally she) wrote, and that 'bias' is a potential source of great importance. It can tell us about that world. Rather than discounting the evidence of clearly political chronicles as propaganda, one can analyse how they set about their projects of legitimation, and the underlying assumptions this reveals. For instance, the very idea of a king can change over time. As Sverre Bagge has shown, through a careful reading of the implicit ideals embedded in certain German chronicles, between the tenth and the twelfth centuries their notion of a good king shifts. In the earlier works, a king is a patron, a warlord and someone protected by God as part of his personal charisma; but, in the mid-eleventh century, the chroniclers start to develop a more 'public' notion of kingship. Distinctions are made between the individual person and the office he holds, and the king governs the people on behalf of God.[24] At no point does any single chronicle set out to explain or reflect upon this change – but it is precisely their implicit, taken-for-granted quality that makes them so valuable to an historian. In this kind of analysis, the 'facts' and opinions that a chronicle provides are less important than the way in which it provides them: the language that it uses, the imagery it deploys and the hidden assumptions about political theory that it reveals.

And those assumptions may well be hidden to the chronicle authors themselves – things that they do not consciously know about themselves and their cultural milieu. As the literary historian Steven Justice has demonstrated, the English chroniclers who recorded the so-called 'Peasant Letters' of 1381 did not understand either the nature or the content of what they had copied down; and their misconceptions were based on a wider set of negative assumptions they held about the peasantry. Precisely by noting this blind spot in the sources,

one can use the prejudice of a text against itself: having identified the manner in which Knighton and Walsingham, in particular, make assumptions about rebel motives and actions,
Justice is able to present a much richer, more nuanced and
greatly sympathetic account of the rising – not by eliminating
their 'biases', but by using them to illuminate those elements
the texts unwittingly let slip.[25] In a parallel fashion, a nuanced
understanding of the gender biases of medieval texts, allied
with a very close and careful reading of the surviving sources,
makes it possible to sketch the underlying role of women as
preservers of family memory, orally passing on stories that
only intermittently make contact with the written record.[26]
It is not, therefore, the case that one must eradicate or over-
come the bias of a chronicler (or, indeed, any other medieval
source); rather, the ways in which medieval culture, politics
and society inflect a particular text provide the historian with
an extremely fertile resource for further research.

Charters

A number of records from ninth-century Brittany survive for
us today, including the following charter, issued on 17 June
860, and recorded in the cartulary of the monastery of Redon:

> Notice of the way in which a man called Uuobrian accused
> another called Uuetenoc about an allod which Uuobrian had
> sold him a long time before. Uuobrian said that he had not sold
> him as much land as he [Uuetenoc] was working. Thereupon
> Uuetenoc raised a court case, gathering his supporters; these
> were called Fomus, Iacu, Rethuualart, Drehuuobri. When his
> charter had been read and his witnesses and sureties had tes-
> tified, it was revealed that all [the land] that he worked had
> been purchased from Uuobrian. Then Uuobrian, vanquished
> as much by the charter as by the witnesses and guarantors,
> confessed. This was done in Ruffiac church, on the 15th kal-
> ends July, Monday, before Machtiern Iarnhitin and Hinuualart
> and Litoc, the representative of Princeps Salomon, and before
> many noble men [. . . names listed]. Eusorchit [a cleric] then
> read the charter in public, to the effect that all had been sold to
> Uuetenoc just as he had said from his own charter.[27]

What is a charter? In broad terms, it is the record of an agreement, whether of the transfer of land or other property from one party to another, the settlement of a dispute, or the bestowal of certain rights.[28] The first two cases are included in the example above: the charter itself records the settlement of a dispute, in this case in a legal setting, and it mentions the existence of an earlier charter between Uuobrian and Uuetenoc recording the original sale of the disputed allod. What was transferred by charter did not necessarily have to be land, however, nor was it necessarily something 'sold' by one person to another. Duke Henry of Sandomierz issued a charter in 1166 to a monastery at Zagosc in Poland, stating: 'I give [the monks] the tavern in Czechów in order [to enable them] to restore the oxen in the said villages . . . No one may presume to inflict any injury on, or demand any service from, the taverner whom [the monks] should establish at Czechów.'[29] Duke Henry was transferring the income and control of the tavern to the monastery, while implicitly retaining certain rights of lordship over the taverner (and possibly also a future reassertion of ownership of the property itself); and he was not selling it to the monastery but donating it as a gift. Nor did charters recording the settlement of disputes necessarily have to be produced by courts. A Catalan document from around 990 records that one Ramió, having realized that a certain Julius had been stealing bread and wine from him, decided not to take Julius to court, but to make a private agreement, part of which committed Ramió and his descendants to refraining from any future prosecution – a record of this promise being a primary purpose for creating the document.[30] Finally, charters were used not only by private individuals, but at the very highest levels of society: medieval towns and cities petitioned kings and princes for a charter establishing their rights to act independently as civic entities, usually allowing them freedom from certain kinds of taxation, the exercise of legal jurisdiction and other specific matters. Many English towns 'gained their charter' in the twelfth century, setting them on a course for civic expansion in that and the following century. The most famous charter for the anglophone world is probably the Magna Carta ('Great Charter') issued by King John at Runnymede in 1215, which sets out fundamental rights in English common law, along with sundry other matters such as the removal of all fish-weirs from the Thames and Medway and the king agreeing not to sequester other nobles' timber.

Collections of charters – cartularies – are one of the richest medieval sources for the early middle ages, and indeed beyond. The majority of what survives relates to monasteries, because they had the means and desire to archive such records over long periods of time; in the case of Uuobrian and Uuetenoc, the latter donated the land under dispute to the monastery some five years later, and hence the monks of Redon wished to keep a record of the earlier charter in case of future argument. There is some evidence to suggest that in certain areas of early medieval Europe, lay people also made archives (albeit often still storing them in monasteries or churches), and recent work suggests that this may originally have happened on a larger scale than we have hitherto tended to imagine.[31] There is possibly a very slight hint of this in the mention of the earlier charter that Uuetenoc brought to court, in the case from Brittany: clearly someone had kept this document because of its potential future importance.

Charters touch upon elements of the lives and activities of people from many different social levels, and by 1300, as Michael Clanchy has shown, charters were being regularly used for land transfer in England even between peasants.[32] They are therefore a hugely valuable kind of document, containing information about people, places, properties and practices – although, in each of these cases, care is needed in exactly how one uses the information a charter presents. To take a very simple example, charters that contain information about land donations – a primary feature in monastic cartularies – can allow us to map the extent, growth or diminution, value and geographical patterns of monastic landholding. By looking at the people making the donations, historians have discussed patterns of pious giving among social elites. In other words, one can look at who gave what to whom. However, matters may be more complex than this initially makes clear. The nature of donations, and the rights they provided over the land given, could vary, and could indeed be subject to future dispute. It is unlikely, to return to the case of Duke Henry and the Zagosc monks, that the duke intended the monastery to be able to do anything it wanted with the tavern in perpetuity, only that it could have the income to restore its flocks. Beyond that indeterminate point, the matter became hazy: the monastery would likely retain the income unless the duke, or another party, made a future claim – but if it attempted to sell the tavern to a third party, it could find the matter subject to dispute by the duke or his heirs. Whether or not one sees 'dispute' behind every property transfer, it is certainly the case that land donated to monasteries seems to have sometimes been handed back and forth between the family of the donator and the recipients, the same piece of land somehow being 'given' at various points in time. What was transferred by charter is not always as obvious as one might first think.

Study of monastic holdings also needs to beware of forgery, something far from unusual when dealing with monastic charters. As documents became more essential in the establishment of rights, monasteries had a habit of producing helpful charters, often 'backdated' several centuries, in defence of their claims. Nor were monks the only culprits: the city of Marseille, claiming Montpellier as a subject territory in a series of cases heard before the pope in the mid-thirteenth century, conveniently 'discovered' charters dating to 1136, 1152, 1163 and 1198 setting out its rights, all of which are now considered to be forgeries.[33] Another possibility regarding Uuctcnoc's 'earlier' charter in the Redon dispute is that this was a forgery produced in order to bolster the case against Uuobrian.

The very nature of 'giving' can also be complex. Anthropological work on gifts has long suggested that an element of reciprocity is usually involved: one gives because one expects to get something back; or, one gives because one wishes to place the recipient in one's debt; or further, one gives precisely because the recipient is unable to give back (or give as much), and therefore one can show off relative wealth and power. Barbara Rosenwein's work on gifts of land to the monastery of Cluny in the tenth and eleventh centuries has demonstrated how many of these transactions were about other matters than the actual land itself. The same pieces of land can be found being gifted and re-gifted over time, with little clear sense of 'ownership' as one might expect from a modern property market. Instead, Rosenwein suggests, property transactions acted as a kind of 'social glue' in a period arguably marked by the fragmentation of authority. Making gifts was a way of connecting oneself with the monastery, and vice versa.[34] An essential technique in pursuing this kind of analysis has been prosopography: the tracking of individuals across multiple documents, tracing kinship networks between those individuals (and, in Rosenwein's case, mapping the areas of land mentioned in the charters). Work on the people mentioned in charters – not only the primary individuals, but the various witnesses and others – has demonstrated just how much one can extract from seemingly sparse information. The order in which witnesses appear in charter lists, the recurrence or otherwise of witnesses across charters, can be used to suggest something of the social fabric behind the charter, its lines of connection, tension and power.

This is true too of the narrative details that some charters contain. Take the charter concerning Uuobrian and Uuetenoc. Just these short lines provide a glimpse of various important themes. The fact that Uuetenoc, the accused, rather than Uuobrian, the accuser, brought the case to court indicates that one might choose to use the law, rather than have it forced upon one; it probably also suggests that he had connections to Salomon, a major source of power in the region. Something of the social setting of the law, and its methods, is also suggested. The case involved the presence of a representative of the prince, and other noble men, but took place in the local church: a combination of secular and ecclesiastical authority. The court heard testimony from witnesses (though whether they were giving evidence on the objective facts, or on the character of the protagonists, is not clear), and heard the contents of an earlier charter – it being this written evidence as much as the oral testimony that brought the verdict in Uuetenoc's favour. Indeed, something the charter indicates is the interpenetration of orality and literacy: the written word carried weight and importance, alongside oral testimony, but the charters also had to be read aloud (as the cleric Eusorchit reads the charter itself, in conclusion to the matter) to be made 'public'. The study of more charters, over a longer period of time, would allow us to map the contours of these areas in greater detail; and we would likely find a shift from more oral to more literate ways of dealing with property and evidence, the development of other kinds of courts and legal jurisdictions that separated ecclesiastical from secular, and other changes in documentary practice. Studies of further disputes and their settlements have similarly allowed historians to track patterns of ritual behaviour, lines of social power, and methods by which individuals negotiated their relative position in society.

In all these areas, and more, it is good to think of charters as being more than passive reflections and records of past events. Civic charters were important as symbols as much as for the detail they contained; as Brigitte Bedos-Rezak has shown, French towns reproduced their charters in multiple forms, by making beautifully illuminated copies or by pretending that an earlier copy had been lost and petitioning the requisite lord for another duplicate.[35] The ability to create and archive authoritative written materials was in itself a demonstration of power – for monasteries, for royal chanceries and, in the later middle ages, for towns and cities. Charters were little repositories of useful memory, ready to be deployed tactically in future disputes. This was, of course, the very reason that charters were kept. The way in which the record was made, the function of the written record, was therefore active rather than passive: charters did things, or, at least, had the potential to do things, if not at the moment of their creation then in the future.[36] As we will see further below, this point can be expanded to all the sources of the period: a document was not a reflection so much as an action.

Images

The medieval images most familiar to us today are either very large, such as the stained glass in Chartres Cathedral, or else really quite small, as is the case with most manuscript illuminations. These are, at both extremes, also rather specialized kinds of images. Chartres was a wondrous creation even in the thirteenth century, intended from its very inception to impress and awe the viewer. Manuscript illuminations were for the most part only seen by the kinds of people who illuminated manuscripts, namely monks, or (in the fourteenth and fifteenth centuries) those who bought them, namely very rich people. These images remain useful, but others are also important, and more truly ubiquitous: the images stamped onto coins or embedded in seals, for example, or the simpler pictures painted onto parish church walls or carved into parish church rood screens. It is true that, from the late fourteenth century, illuminated manuscripts in the form of books of hours reached a wider, secular audience; but these were still largely the possession of social elites, and their relative ubiquity should not be extended into a general sense of 'popular' culture. The religious image that ordinary people in the Christian West would probably have seen most often was the cross in the form of two intersecting lines: this simple image has been found carved into bedheads, onto loaves, over lintels and in other quotidian settings.[37] It was an action as much as an image, since 'making the sign of the cross' was something taught to all Christians in childhood.

The analysis of images presents a number of potential pitfalls for the historian, some purely technical, some more interpretative and epistemological.[38] At a technical level, medieval art employed a variety of semiotic devices to communicate meaning, and one must be able to decode these to make sense of an image. The precise way in which someone's fingers are depicted was intended, for example, to tell the viewer what the person was doing: listening, arguing, blessing, preaching, and so forth. Different medieval saints have particular objects associated with them, through which one could identify the figure – St Katherine's wheel, St Michael's sword – and, at a less exalted level, the coats of arms of late medieval noblemen played a similar role. Colour was important, in many different ways, and often contextually within a particular image.[39] Different religious orders, and different kinds of clergy, wore robes of identifying colours (in reality as well as in pictures). The relative positions of people within an image represented their relationships and hierarchy.

These may seem daunting matters; in fact, they are for the most part fairly straightforward technical considerations, and considerable help in decoding details can be gleaned from reference books.[40] What matters as much as reading the language of the picture is thinking – as one must do for any source – about its precise context and function. For example, pictures painted onto church walls are sometimes assumed to have been used to instruct the laity in their faith, possibly as kinds of visual aids to preaching. One can certainly make wonderful use of images of this kind in deepening our sense of the imagery evoked within medieval liturgy and religious instruction. For example, Keldby Church, on the Danish island of Møn, is absolutely covered in paintings that depict scenes from the Passion and various other biblical events and figures. In one area of the nave, two kneeling sinners pray at the foot of the Crucifixion, one contemplating Christ's wounds, the other distracted by worldly things, demonstrated by lines linking him to various objects such as his horse, his clothing and a housewife tasting the stew she is tending in her cooking pot, a domestic scene that would presumably have looked extremely familiar to the congregation.[41] The pictures in the choir at Keldby date to the late thirteenth century, while most of those in the nave are from the fourteenth and fifteenth centuries; however, only the latter would have been easily visible to the laity. Work elsewhere similarly suggests that we should therefore not in fact assume that images were always for lay instruction: some thirteenth-century churches in France only had paintings on the walls of the apse, not the nave, the details of which were visible only to the clergy. The laity would have seen the fact of the images, but not the images themselves; their lesson was hence more that of clerical privilege and hierarchy than theological detail.[42] Equally, art that might appear to be private and domestic – for instance, Andrea Mantegna's fresco (1465–74) for the marquis of Mantua's private chamber – could in fact be 'public', as something that visitors specifically requested to see, due to its fame.[43] Medieval images could be intended to impress, to inspire, to provide models for good conduct, to be meditated on, to be laughed at, to signal identity and status, to narrate, to scare. The creators of these images drew upon artistic convention, classical and biblical narrative, specific semiotic codes, the desires of their patrons, the available resources – and, sometimes, what they saw around them.

The search for the latter has often been the object of historical (as opposed to art historical) study. Images can provide a lot of important information about the minutiae of medieval life. Various technical medical practices are illustrated in manuscripts, such as cataract surgery, bloodletting and urine analysis. The tools and methods of particular trades – carpentry, goldsmithery, butchery, brewing – can be seen, corroborating textual and archaeological evidence. Some sense of the visual impact of markets and fairs, civic processions and plays, funerals and sacramental rituals can be drawn from visual materials of various kinds. All of this is extremely valuable. But one must be wary. Past historians had a bad habit of taking details from medieval literature as 'straight' depictions of life at the time, without regard to textual context or the stylistic devices of medieval authors (including irony, satire, anachronism, genre convention and the tropological expectations of narrative).

A similar problem can befall those using images. Take, for example, a famous set of images, the book of hours known as *Les Très Riches Heures du Duc de Berry*. Look at the picture illustrating the month of February (see Figure 2.2). In the bottom left, we see a simple hut, three seated figures warming themselves at the fire. Look closely at the smaller two: their genitalia are clearly visible, if curiously hairless. Clear circumstantial evidence that medieval people wore nothing under their outer garments (and were prepubescent for many years)? Or a visual joke about bare-arsed peasants and their crudity? Given that many of the calendar illustrations juxtapose courtly finery with peasant simplicity, something of the latter is probably more likely; though what exactly is open to argument.[44]

In recent decades, however, historians using images have been less interested in the pursuit of physical details, and more interested in the ways in which images might relate to how people thought about things. The Mappa Mundi, a world map made in thirteenth-century Hereford, tells us little about the actual world (two of the continents are missing) but quite a lot about how some people thought about the world. Looking at the Mappa Mundi, one learns about relative perceptual geographies (England, its place of creation, is curiously large); the boundaries between the known and the unknown or the ordered centre and disordered peripheries (the latter, in the north and east, populated by monstrous races); and the overarching theological framework within which existence is set (Christ at the heart of the world in

Figure 2.2 *Les Très Riches Heures du Duc de Berry*, month of February (Wikimedia Commons)

Jerusalem, and Christ also overarching the world at the top of the map). Images of Christ of various kinds, compared across the centuries, indicate a general shift in depiction, from Christ in potent majesty, to Christ as the Man of Sorrows, suffering very bodily torment on the cross. An element of this relates to artistic convention, but in aggregate it clearly suggests a shift in how Jesus was thought about, and which elements in the Christian message were deemed most powerful at different points in time.

Like the other sources discussed in this chapter, images were active things. They could work to promote and sustain particular ideologies. This was the case with the many repetitious depictions appearing in the later middle ages of Jews as hook-nosed, untrustworthy outsiders, physically bearing the marks of their 'Otherness' to a Christian audience.[45] Images of Jews desecrating Hosts, to accompany stories of the same, worked not only to demonize the Jews but also to emphasize Christ's corporeal presence in that sacrament. Late medieval Italian cities were visually saturated spaces that constantly used images in a complex variety of ways. Apart from religious iconography directed towards catechetical ends, a late medieval Italian might be confronted, while taking a case to law, with a complex and detailed exposition of 'good' and 'bad' forms of government in the form of a vast fresco – a reminder and warning to both citizens and rulers about the necessity of preserving peace, by force if necessary.[46] In a number of Tuscan cities in the thirteenth and fourteenth centuries, criminals (particularly traitors and unscrupulous merchants) who had been prosecuted in absentia and hence eluded the reach of the commune were sometimes punished by *pitture infamanti*: pictures depicting the condemned person were posted up in public places as a kind of visual penalty against their honour.[47] A popular story, appearing in Boccaccio's *Decameron* and elsewhere, of a knight hunting down and eviscerating a naked woman who spurned his advances, was depicted on various late medieval Italian bridal chests that carried the young bride's jewels and clothes into her marriage; a very explicit statement of masculine power and feminine submission.[48] Such images were a form of instruction and also a warning about expected gender roles. One might argue that they 'reflect' social attitudes towards women, but perhaps we should more accurately say that they attempt to construct and police such ideas.

These are all examples of images attempting to wield a fairly direct influence: to carry a particular ideological message. But the functions of images can also be more subtle. Christian art of many different kinds, from wall-paintings to statues to books of hours, worked to evoke emotional and bodily responses in its viewers, playing delicately (or not so delicately) on their feelings. What one felt and thought when looking at Christ crucified could involve a complex weave of associations between the particular image and other works of art, the narrative frameworks for the image rehearsed in sermons, and, for a monastic audience, the texts one might have read reflecting on the very experience one was undergoing.[49] Work yet to be done in this regard concerns the more secular spaces of images: the carvings and signs that adorned medieval civic streets, for example, which can be demonstrated to have their own rich and complex resonances, and are imbricated in different discourses of gender, social order, commerce and control.[50] Pictures can work to frame one's emotional and cognitive response to events in the world: the art historian Mitchell Merback has argued, for example, that late medieval Bohemian images of the two thieves at Christ's crucifixion were linked to contemporary practices of criminal punishment, specifically, breaking people on the wheel. But the nature of the link, Merback emphasizes, is not simply referential, the image 'deriving from' the practice. The images worked, rather, to stimulate the imagination, provide a template joining 'sacred history to familiar reality', evoking a kind of affective knowledge of ideas about penitence; a map for seeing, when in the presence of either the holy image – or the broken body of a common criminal.[51]

Legal Records

'Whoever injures someone with an egg ... should pay ten gold pieces if the plaintiff can prove it.' Thus the law in twelfth-century Castile. The history of law has had a particular importance to medievalists. Frederic W. Maitland, mentioned in Chapter 1 above, was a lawyer and worked on law; and Henry Charles Lea, the great American medievalist historian of inquisition, wrote that 'the surest basis of investigation for a given period [lies] in an examination of its jurisprudence, which presents without disguise its aspirations and the means regarded as best adapted for their realization'.[52] The attractions of law as an historical source are both its provision of fascinating detail – the glimpse of Iberian egg-throwing – and its promise of a larger, more structural system, which might allow one to grapple with society as a whole. Legal records are of course not particular to the study of the middle ages.

But the medieval period has, for most European countries, a foundational place in the establishment of modern legal systems; and some of the records produced by law contain the richest details for aspects of medieval life that would otherwise fall outside the viewpoint of loquacious chroniclers and other such sources. Records of law are also the widest and most varied set of sources discussed in this chapter; indeed, one could count all charters as being legal records. But my focus here is primarily on the kinds of texts produced by the attempted prevention, detection and punishment of crime: law codes, depositions, court judgments, and so forth.

As Lea suggested, law codes can be seen as reflecting a society's aspirations; or, to put it another way, what people worried about and what lay behind those worries. The egg-throwing injunction comes in a section of a law code concerned with honour and violent assault; subsequent items concern 'he who makes up an abusive ballad about another' and 'he who calls someone a leper'.[53] There is a danger here, however, of reading too much purpose and design into medieval law. Law codes often recycled details from older – sometimes much older – records, which means that, just as in modern law, some elements could be misleadingly anachronistic. In the early middle ages, issuing a law code might be seen primarily as a way of indicating that you were the sort of ruler who could issue a law code. Much medieval law – including, for example, that set out in the Magna Carta – was not based on the top-down application of a set of systematic principles, but was something more bottom-up and petitionary.[54] Law came about because a particular issue or problem was raised, a ruler dispensed a judgment, and thus law was written. This was true for both kings and popes. Canon law, the law of the Church for all Christendom, was constructed very largely from responses to petitions, and decisions made about particular situations. Codifications of canon law – most famously Gratian's twelfth-century *Decretum* – were attempts to clarify discordant canons, where those past decisions had reached conflicting conclusions. This perhaps makes medieval law slightly less suitable as a tool for diagnosing the whole structure of a notionally unified society, as Lea imagined it; but at the same time it becomes a tremendously powerful source for information about communal fears and hopes, social tensions and the like.

It can also, from a certain perspective, tell us something about social structure (a topic to which we shall return in Chapter 4): the units and classes into which it imagined society being divided, and the relative rights and status accorded to each. In this sense, what law omits or excludes is often as revealing as what it includes. Certain social ideas are encoded in law, and historians have seen it as particularly revealing in regard to gender. In many European kingdoms, women had a limited place within the law, their ability to litigate or appeal being circumscribed because of their 'changeable' nature, as one fourteenth-century English legal text puts it.[55] Medieval concepts of the crime of rape, albeit not unitary or static on the topic, tended to focus on the injury done to the woman's family rather than herself; and an acceptable reparation was marriage to the perpetrator or the bestowal of a dowry.

Law in practice, as opposed to legal theory, provides an even richer source of material for such matters. To continue with the theme of sexual violence, historians can study the court proceedings for further indications of cultural ideas and attitudes. The usual defence against an accusation of rape was to allege that the woman was a 'common woman', sexually available to all. Examining accounts in these cases provides insight into ideas about honour, gender and sexual double standards. The prosecution of sex crime in late medieval Italy, studied by Guido Ruggiero, demonstrates some of the complexities. The civic authorities used a strongly denunciatory rhetoric in the description of sex crimes – the perpetrator 'dishonouring God' as much as the victim – but their actions did not always follow suit. The rape of single women, in particular, tended to be treated extremely leniently, as a somewhat inevitable and natural fact of social life. Sodomy, however, a crime carrying particular associations of civic instability, was punished harshly.[56] Women's involvement in crime as perpetrators can also tell us things about the world in which they lived. They never numbered more than one-fifth of those prosecuted, probably indicating a real difference in behaviour, and they were rarely charged with homicide. Women did perpetrate violence, but the pattern differed from that of men: other women were the more frequent victims, and they infrequently used weapons.[57]

The uses of legal records are not, however, limited to the history of crime itself. The growth of social history in the 1950s depended particularly upon the study of legal archives, and the development of techniques for mining them effectively as an historical source. Many such texts provide incidental details about the world in which the deponents lived, and these can be invaluable. Barbara Hanawalt has used coroners' rolls to reconstruct a picture of rural life in medieval England; the canonization records (structured similarly to trial dossiers) of St Louis allowed Sharon Farmer to study attitudes towards the poor in thirteenth-century France; Claude Gauvard has analysed themes such as the social construction of space and the construction of community from records of late medieval French royal pardons; and Emmanuel Le Roy Ladurie wrote a detailed study of one village based on very rich inquisitorial records from the early fourteenth century.[58] The social setting of the law itself – the way in which people use courts, and the cultural work that they undertake when so doing – has also recently come under analysis.[59]

Many of the analyses sketched above depend, to a greater or lesser extent, on the numerical analysis of records. This is a powerful tool to which many such sources are suited. The average record of a penance handed out by a thirteenth-century inquisitor could say no more than: 'Coinarc saw Waldensians and heard their preaching. He is to go [on pilgrimage] to [the shrine of] Saint James [of Compostella].'[60] It is hard to do much with a single text of this sort; but given hundreds of them, one can build up a larger picture of those charged by the inquisitor, the penances given, and the shape of heretical activities. In secular law too, while individual cases may be short on detail, the survival of court records over many years encourages an aggregate, statistical approach. But this is not the only way in which the sources can be studied. Trial records often contain narrative information on the crime committed, and one can usefully look not only at the incidental detail contained in such accounts, but at the very shape of the narrative and the way in which it was produced. Those involved in violence will, for obvious reasons, attempt to justify their actions. As Daniel Smail demonstrates for some cases in fourteenth-century Marseille, such justification drew on social norms and could be implicit as much as explicit. For instance, a man called Julian narrated events leading up to the fight he had with another man called Jacme in such a way as to suggest that he was in a hostile part of town, far from any supporting kin, whereas Jacme lived there and was surrounded by potential supporters (both these facts being false, as subsequent evidence revealed); and that Jacme had earlier that year assaulted one of Julian's kin, thus making Julian's attack on Jacme a matter of feud, and hence legitimate. These details were not glossed with such meanings in the record; they were, rather, embedded within the story that Julian told.[61]

Many court cases were petitionary rather than prosecutorial: one or both disputants chose to go to law (or, quite frequently, to appeal an earlier decision to a higher court). A principal way in which such sources have been used is the study of dispute settlement, an area of enquiry much influenced by anthropological theory and extending beyond the formal bounds of law.[62] Sources of law can, in this way, show us something about sociocultural tensions and relations. But a good proportion of records, including the inquisition registers used by Le Roy Ladurie and the civic trials studied by Ruggiero, were the product of top-down prosecution, the application of legal force from above. In these cases, historians are allowed different analytical possibilities, such as the ways in which people resisted (or otherwise) the imposition of legal forms on their lives. James Given's study of medieval inquisition has examined, for example, how people individually attempted to elude the religious authorities, and collectively disrupt their activities, through burning their archives or other acts of violence. The coercive context of these kinds of trial raises further questions about the ways in which the narratives of the sources were produced, as the inquisitor attempted to apply a particular framework of classification to the witness, and the witness (on occasion) negotiated the experience as best as he or she was able.[63]

Talk of inquisition raises a final possibility for the use of legal sources and the law: what they reveal of changing ideas about truth and enquiry. Inquisition (*inquisitio*) is a form of legal procedure, applied particularly to the prosecution of heresy in the thirteenth century but also used as the main legal form in much late medieval secular law, apart from in England. *Inquisitio* allowed judges to proceed directly against suspected crimes on the basis of *fama* (rumour/public knowledge), through an investigatory procedure. In this, it largely replaced earlier legal forms such as *accusatio*, which required a specific individual to bring an accusation to the court's attention; and the period when *inquisitio* rose to prominence – the early thirteenth century – also saw the decline of the trial by ordeal, whereby the accused could prove his innocence by being relatively unharmed after holding a red-hot iron or some similar test. As these legal forms shifted, the relationships between God, the community and law were refashioned, and historians are still arguing about how best to interpret these changes. What constituted 'truth' within a legal setting was always to some extent a communal matter – the decision of a jury, or a group of oath-swearers, or bound by social expectations of narrative and memory – but *inquisitio* also brought with it the active use of the archive, as witnesses' statements were checked against others, and records were used to catch out past transgressions and shape the possibility of future ones. In this sense, legal records embodied as much as reflected power. The historian's archive is not innocent: it once did things, to real people.

3
Reading the Middle Ages

The annual migrations of European and American medievalists, though slightly contrasting, follow an essentially similar pattern. Every spring, a vast number of the Americans,
some 3,000 or 4,000-strong, both young and old, flock in
haste from all over the US to a large town in Michigan –
Kalamazoo – home to a state university, a lovely but underpa-
tronized museum of local history, and some rather nice bars.
There, perched cheek-by-jowl in rooms of almost monastic
simplicity, they hold a congress. This involves a great, exciting, interwoven babble of discussion, argument and gossip,
and the obsessive purchasing of books to take back home
to their nests. At the end of four intense days, they depart
as swiftly as they arrived. In the early summer, across the
Atlantic, a very similar phenomenon can be observed, this
time centred on the English city of Leeds. More languages are
spoken at Leeds (Polish, Dutch, German, a little French and
Japanese) in addition to the native English, and there are only
two bars, but otherwise the behaviour is much the same.

The International Congress on Medieval Studies at
Kalamazoo (begun in 1966) and the International Medieval
Congress at Leeds (begun in 1994), to give them more respect-
fully their proper titles, are not, of course, the only conferences
that medievalists organize or attend. Many other annual and
occasional events are held across the world; in the year in
which I first wrote this book, one found them on topics as

broad as 'Power' and as specific as 'The Battle of Tinchebray, 1106'. Nor by any means do all medievalists attend Leeds or Kalamazoo: other European countries have their own meetings, medievalists attend cross-chronology conferences, and some prefer to shun the large jamborees altogether. But these two annual talk-fests are currently the largest gatherings of medievalist minds. And they share a notable feature in comparison to other historical colloquia: both sprang from and continue to embrace interdisciplinary study of the middle ages. Neither is purely a historical or literary conference (or for that matter, archaeological or art historical). Medievalists have grown very used to working across and between apparent disciplinary boundaries.

This does not mean that no such boundaries exist, and I shall explore some points of tension below. But all disciplines are agreed that the middle ages, by dint of the nature and fragmentary survival of the evidence, benefits hugely by approaching it from a range of perspectives. Thus, in discussing medieval history, one must note that it is frequently a kind of history in conversation (both collaborative and argumentative) with other approaches; and, increasingly frequently, that it draws upon cognitive tools developed in other parts of academia. Art history I mentioned in the previous chapter. Archaeology, science, and some other tools drawn from the social sciences and the study of literature, are discussed below. First, however, we must turn to probably the biggest influence: anthropology.

Anthropology

The Catalan writer Ramon Muntaner (1264–c.1330) begins his vernacular chronicle with an account not of the birth but of the conception of King Jaime I of Aragon in 1207. King Pedro II, Muntaner tells us, had grown bored with his wife Maria of Montpellier, and had a roving eye for other courtly ladies. This 'much afflicted and displeased' the nobility and people of Montpellier, and all the more so when Pedro set his sights on another woman from the area. Thus a deception was formulated: the king would be invited to the lady's darkened bedchamber, but with his wife substituted in the place of her latest rival. In the week leading up to the ruse, all the priests in the area said masses in praise of the Virgin Mary, and on the Saturday, the people of Montpellier fasted. That night, as the king lay with his woman, the people went to church and prayed; and outside the chamber door, throughout the night, there knelt in prayer 'twenty-four notables and abbots and priors and the bishop's clerks and religious, and the twelve [most honourable] ladies and the twelve damsels, with tapers in their hands', and also two notaries.

> And the king and queen rested together, and the lord king believed he had at his side the lady of whom he was enamoured ... And when it was dawn, all the notables ... each with their lighted taper in their hand, entered the chamber; and the lord king was in his bed with the queen, and wondered [at this intrusion], and sprang up at once on the bed and seized his sword. And all knelt down and said weeping: 'Lord, deign to look and see who it is lies by your side.' And the queen sat up and the lord king recognized her; and they told him all they had disposed. And the lord king said that, since it was so, might it please God to fulfil their intention.

Pedro left Montpellier the next day, but six knights and their wives and damsels stayed with the queen for the following nine months, until Jaime I, conceived that night, was born. The two notaries 'in the presence of the king' wrote 'public letters of the event, writing that same night'.[1]

What does one do with such a tale? A hard-headed historian attempting to reconstruct a narrative of important events might well be tempted simply to ignore it, treat it as meaningless background 'noise', while continuing a search for hard facts. After all, the combination of miracles and narrative implausibility makes it hard to take as a true story. Another approach might note it as a mark of characteristically medieval simplicity and credulity. But both tactics would surely leave us a little disappointed: must we either diagnose these medieval people as simpletons, or else abandon all attempts to interpret? It is at this conceptual point that anthropology has come helpfully into play.

One of the earliest, and certainly most influential, uses of anthropological ideas was indeed in a ground-breaking attempt to interpret what previous generations of historians had seen as curious but essentially meaningless beliefs surrounding medieval monarchs. Marc Bloch's *Les Rois thaumaturges* (1924; English translation *The Royal Touch*, 1973) dealt with the practice of kings curing scrofula by laying hands on the afflicted, something found from the thirteenth to the eighteenth century. In taking such a topic seriously – and indeed arguing that it illuminated extremely important aspects of royal power, image-making and pre-modern authority – Bloch was influenced by the work of the anthropologist Lucien Lévy-Bruhl and the sociologist Émile Durkheim. The former gave him the tools to consider whether a pre-modern society and culture ('primitive' in Lévy-Bruhl's terms) could have a different, but internally coherent, way of thinking and acting from a modern one; its own *mentalité*, to use the Annaliste term. Durkheim's work encouraged Bloch to see the ritual and symbolic elements of sovereignty as important: part of 'collective representations' that informed the very functioning of society itself.[2] Something like the 'royal touch' was, for Bloch, not simply a piece of royal propaganda disseminated from the top down, but part of a collective social idea about hierarchy, intervention and structure. Indeed, 'structure' was at the heart of his, and later Annaliste, analyses – and similarly in anthropology. In treating Muntaner's narrative of Jaime I's arrival into this world in a structuralist way, one might note the shared set of values across social hierarchies (all 'the people', as well as the notables and bishops, are engaged in prayer for a successful outcome), while also seeing how structural subdivisions of those hierarchies allotted different kinds of roles to different sorts of people, with a concomitant belief that the collective whole, through which society functioned, was more important than any individual role. Even the king, in this sense, was part of the structure, rather than hovering above it: while placatory in their confrontation with him, it is clear that the nobles specifically, and the city in general, required Pedro to play an allotted role, and manipulated him to precisely this end. Another structural element – the idea of honour, and its link to both place (Montpellier) and kin (the noble families) – is key to understanding the story.

The structuralist anthropology of Durkheim and other later figures, such as Claude Lévi-Strauss, Marcel Mauss and Victor Turner, was hugely influential, particularly on French

medievalists. Georges Duby found in Mauss ways of understanding the central role of gift exchange in early medieval
economies and politics; something that has continued to provide a fruitful line of enquiry for later medievalists.[3] Inspired
by Lévi-Strauss and others, Jacques Le Goff has pursued a
variety of symbolic elements in medieval culture – notions
of 'wilderness', the meanings of marvels, the importance and
interpretation of gesture, the different conceptions of 'time'
embodied in ecclesiastical and mercantile cultures.[4] Victor
Turner has been influential on studies of medieval religion
(about which he himself wrote), particularly in his analysis of
rites of passage and what he calls 'liminality' – a borderland
condition, marked by elements of role-reversal and fluidity,
which engenders both charismatic power and collective cohesion.[5] Liminality has been a useful conceptual tool in understanding the ways in which medieval saints and holy people
are produced, either in reality or in narrative. Both Francis
of Assisi and Waldes of Lyon, for example, came from rich
mercantile backgrounds, and underwent sudden reversals
of condition through illness and voluntary impoverishment,
leading to accusations of madness as they stepped 'outside'
society, only to then be reintegrated as leaders of groups (the
Franciscans and the Waldensian heretics, respectively), and
emerge as charismatic leaders, facilitating social cohesion.
The theory has been further adapted and critiqued in regard
to female saints, whose social position was arguably always
already 'liminal' by dint of their sex.[6] Peter Brown, an influential historian of late antiquity, has developed analyses of
the social function of holy men (and occasionally women) in
his period, in an anthropological fashion that has provided
further models for discussion.[7] In each case, the anthropology
allows one to go beyond noting the fact of religious belief to
think more about its social effects, its psychic affects, its narrative conventions – and hence to understand more about the
social and cultural work that religion performs.

   Another area where anthropological work – principally
that by Jack Goody and Walter Ong – has been hugely
important is in the study of medieval literacy and orality.
For Goody, societies that were not dominated by literacy and
texts (including, he would argue, the early middle ages) are
characterized by an 'oral' culture that differs in various ways

from literate culture. Orality, Goody suggested, is more fluid, transitory and labile, whereas literacy fixes things – customs, laws, norms – into static positions, and hence facilitates the development of further complexities.[8] As European society undeniably did move from a lesser to a greater degree of literacy over the long medieval period – although the degree to which the early middle ages lacked literacy is debatable – there is an obvious attraction to thinking about what differences the presence or absence of the technology of writing made to societies. Some have seen signs of a cultural cleavage between the literate clerical elite and the oral mass populace, played out in various ways and with various effects (something to which I shall return in the following chapter). The idea of thinking of literacy as more than a skill, as something encoding a number of cultural investments, has prompted further analyses. As mentioned in the opening pages of this book, *litteratus* in the medieval West meant Latin literacy, and moreover the implication of a particular cognitive authority and ability. Literacy was something contested in medieval societies. Two ninth-century Byzantine priests were sent by their emperor to preach Christianity to the Slavs of Moravia. To aid their conversionary task, they developed (for the first time) a written form of Slavic, and translated the Greek bible and some other texts into that language. However, when visiting Venice and Salzburg, despite their efforts to aid the spread of Christianity, the priests were attacked by Carolingian clerics for their translation activities.[9] For the western clergy at that time, there were only three sacred languages: Greek, Hebrew and Latin. Anything else defamed God's word. In practice, Latin had become the language of western Christianity, and hence a foreign language to northern Europe. Moreover, within the Carolingian empire – and then more widely, into the German lands, Poland, Hungary and Scandinavia – Latin became also the language of kingship and secular authority. Literacy was not an inert medium; it was deeply implicated in structures of power. Concomitantly, some historians have discussed oral cultures of resistance, seeking to demonstrate different modes of cultural operation – in memorialization, dispute settlement, feud, and so forth – rooted in a cognitively different mode from that dictated by textual culture.

However, the ideas of Goody and Ong also point to some

of the potential pitfalls of the use of anthropology. Some historians have doubts about the applicability of theories based on the observation of, say, mid-twentieth-century Polynesian tribes, to, say, fifteenth-century Waldensian heretics. Moreover, the 'literacy thesis' of Goody has been comprehensively criticized within anthropology for its essentialism and nativism – the assumption of a 'simplicity' to oral cultures, and the inherent teleologism of seeing literacy as a 'development'.[10] More broadly, some older strains of anthropology, based on a view of 'native' society as 'primitive', have unhappily bolstered views of the middle ages (particularly the early middle ages) as similarly basic – as a kind of historical 'childhood' out of which modern society 'grew up'. But as recent work demonstrates, in both the anthropology of oral cultures and the history of the early middle ages, societies that lack textual records are not simple, but in fact highly complex – only that complexity is less apparent to the historian's or anthropologist's first glance. With specific regard to medieval literacy, historians have more recently argued for the interpenetration of oral and literate modes of culture, noting for example the ability of one literate person to disseminate a text to a much wider circle (hence expanding the practical effect of literacy), while also pointing to the particular cultural 'charge' that literacy and texts carried with them in the middle ages.[11] One might note here the presence of both in Ramon Muntaner's world: the importance of the two scribes at the apparent impregnation of Maria of Montpellier – literacy – balanced against the importance of the large and various numbers of personal witnesses also present – orality, of a paralegal nature. (One could further note that while Muntaner was producing a vernacular chronicle that stood in relation to other historical texts, he was almost certainly reliant upon oral tradition for his source of this particular story; and the tale itself reverses a much older story told of attempts to replace the lawful wife of King Pippin the Short (751–68) with another woman.)

Where historians, particularly anglophone medievalists, have been most cautious about anthropology is in regard to the latter discipline's search for deep structuring principles in human social formations. While this appealed to Bloch's generation of historians, and many of the French medievalists who came after him, it has been treated much more warily by English, American and German historians, who have seen their job as dealing more with specificities than with generalities. However, anthropology itself moved on in the second half of the twentieth century. The 'anthropology (or sociology) of the everyday', associated particularly with Pierre Bourdieu and Michel de Certeau, has provided a further set of analytical tools, 'poststructuralist' in the sense that they do not assume the presence of deep, stable structures in human affairs, but see rather more contingent, fluid and ideological structuring principles that ebb and flow in different situations.[12] Bourdieu presents the notion of *habitus*, the set of embodied practices that encode a social group's ideological principles 'below' the level of overt discussion: in medieval terms, for example, the combination of public behaviour and gossip that constitutes *fama* ('fame' or 'rumour' or 'honour', depending on the situation).[13] Bourdieu encourages one to see the logic of apparently inexplicable or barbarous social events from the historical actor's point of view, within the shared systems of their cultural context. William Miller thus demonstrates the coherence of feuds within medieval Icelandic culture, excavating the complex set of ideas about 'exchange', economic or symbolic, within which feuding made sense.[14]

The best of medieval historiography – Miller being an excellent example – talks back to anthropology, furthering discussion and development of the analytical tools that both disciplines use in their attempts to grapple with human societies. And anthropology is perhaps best understood not simply as a provider of 'models' of behaviour that can be taken to the medieval archive, but as a prompt to new questions, rooted particularly in anthropology's willingness to listen to what 'the Other' has to say, and take it seriously on its own terms. Thus, recent medieval work has begun to think about the ideological formation of social space, modes of acculturation, the uses of gift exchange, the social construction of emotions, and other such topics. There are problems with the direct application of anthropological models here, not least because anthropologists can talk with the subjects of their analysis – a rather key element in the study of emotions, for example – whereas historians can only read/see/excavate the traces of their subjects. But, given that the starting point for historians is the initial encounter with the evidence – the discovery of Muntaner's tale of Jaime I's conception, for example – anthropology continues to provide essential help in developing the right kinds of questions to ask, and the most productive attitude of sympathetic enquiry in which to ask them.

Numbers and Statistics

Ramon Muntaner's chronicle posed one kind of problem – how to get inside a story from a world not completely like our own. But other kinds of evidence present different challenges. Take, for example, the Florentine *catasto* of 1427. This was a highly detailed and diligent tax assessment survey of the city and its subject environs, carried out in response to the city's ongoing economic problems caused by war with Milan. A fiscal head of household was noted in the survey, and assessment made of not only property value (assessed by its economic productiveness) but also business investments, and holdings in the city's public debt. The records supply other details too: the number of people in each household, the name of the fiscal head and usually his or her occupation, the location of the household and its holdings, and so forth. It is, in other words, a very rich record. And vast: nearly ten thousand entries for the city itself, and more for the *contado* and *distretto* (the countryside around Florence and the areas beyond).

This is not a document that presents a narrative, tells of people's feelings or proffers words allegedly said by a startled king in his bedchamber. It is more like looking at a modern telephone book: a daunting mass of data, with no obvious immediate use beyond that for which it was created. It is here that other kinds of skills and tools come into use, those drawn from economic history. We should note at the outset two broadly different aspects of economics that medieval historians, among others, have found useful: first, economic theory (such as Marxism), which seeks to explain, often on a grand scale, the course of human events primarily through underlying economic causes; second, the tools of serial analysis and statistics. That is, plotting the movement of certain variables over time (often via graphs), and condensing large bodies of data into meaningful and comparative proportions (often via tables). Thus, although one cannot 'read' the *catasto* in any meaningful, linear fashion as one might read a chronicle or a sermon, one can make it speak in all kinds of interesting ways, about not only tax but also neighbourhood, lifecycle, gender, and other matters. We do this not by reading, but by counting.

The tax survey – and others like it, in Italy and elsewhere (although the 1427 *catasto* is probably the richest medieval record of its kind) – can be analysed first for proportionate relationships in various ways: social roles, gender, household size, geographical location, and so forth. David Herlihy and Christine Klapisch-Zuber did just this, and more, in their important book *Les Toscans et leurs familles* (1978), and they tackled the huge pile of information the *catasto* contains by creating a database. The various pieces of information gathered by the tax officials were placed in different fields, and one can then search across these fields, singly or in combination, to construct different statistical pictures. Some of this database (relating only to the city) is now online, and, treading in Herlihy and Klapisch-Zuber's footsteps, we can attempt to ask questions of it ourselves.[15] Let's think about what size a household was, according to whether one owned or rented the accommodation. At each stage, we ask the database a specific question – how many entries of this kind, of that kind? How many entries mentioning this, but not that? – and then try to consider the contextual variables that need to be taken into account. The online database tells us that 4,111 heads of household declared that they owned the house in which they lived, whereas 4,196 said they rented (the remainder – 377, mostly servants or grandparents who, for some reason, were being treated as the fiscal head for the purposes of the *catasto* – lived in houses where they did not pay rent). Of these, 1,278 of the owner-occupied houses had households of six or more people, whereas only 915 of the renters were as large as this. The disparity grows as one moves to larger household sizes: 636 of the owners had eight or more people in their house, compared to 334 renters. If one looks for very large households – ten or more people – there are still 276 owners in this position, whereas only 111 renters made it into double figures. Given a total number of households of this large size – 402 – the owners thus constituted 68.7 per cent of very large households, against 27.6 per cent of the renters (the small remainder being houses of non-owning, non-rent payers). Of course, these were still a minority within the city: households of ten or more people formed less than 5 per cent of Florence's dwellings, only 6 per cent of owners had these very large households, and only 2 per cent of renters.

One could continue playing with such figures for some time, and they would probably make best sense plotted on a graph for each value of household size, rather than the slightly arbitrary divisions that I've chosen here. The 377 non-renters ought also to be further analysed – although mathematical techniques exist for establishing how much their returns could potentially affect the figures given. But in any case, the broad point is made: large households in Florence in 1427 were more likely to be found in properties owned by the occupiers. The important thing to note for us – as this is not a book about fifteenth-century Florence or medieval household structures – is that through using certain tools of analysis, a forbiddingly detailed record like the *catasto* can be made to speak. Of course, my brief investigation here is but a beginning: one wants to know why household size varied thus – the greater presence of family elders, larger numbers of children, or greater numbers of servants? – and this would involve asking further specific questions of the *catasto* and also looking at other evidence for fifteenth-century Florence such as household diaries or letters.

The *catasto* of 1427 allows us to investigate that city synchronically – that is, take a momentary slice through time – but bringing other evidence into play permits diachronic analysis: asking questions about change over time. Samuel Cohn, for example, has used the 1427 *catasto* in conjunction with seven other sets of taxation records, stretching from 1365 to 1460, to examine ten Tuscan villages, comparing the demographic and economic experiences between the mountains and the plains, how they changed during the period, and paying particular attention to the experience of women (which, he argues, became progressively harder).[16] And it is not only fiscal records that can be usefully examined in this way:

Cohn has also used statistical analysis of Italian wills to study patterns of testamentary culture and how they changed over time, arguing from this data that fourteenth-century plague (but more the return of plague in 1363 than the initial 'Black Death' of 1348–51) affected the manner in which Italians disposed of their property and moveables after death.[17] Other historians have used statistics to analyse matters as varied as the gender of medieval saints, patterns of criminal behaviour, the preaching practices of heretics, the contours of monastic kinship networks, the mortality rate of monks during plague, and so on. If you can count it, you can analyse it statistically.

When using statistical and serial analyses, one needs to remember the nature of the evidence base. The *catasto* provides but one set of information, and other sources (where they exist) may add nuance to the picture of Florentine society, and could alter it substantially. Drawing graphs and tables is fantastically useful, as a means of generating usable information from large datasets; but, through its numerical and graphical nature, it can start to look beguilingly 'factual'. For example, any study of wills – a form of evidence often subjected to statistical analysis – must be framed by the fact that only a proportion of medieval wills survive for any single area, and many lower social groups never made wills in the first place. Therefore, claims made about testamentary culture reflect the practices of only part of the population – that part visible to us from this kind of evidence. When conducting serial analyses of change over time, the historian needs records that provide the same or very similar data across a number of years. Studies on the economic effects of the Black Death have, for example, used manorial records to look at changes in wages in later fourteenth-century England. Any analysis of wage fluctuation must, first of all, be set alongside price fluctuation to give it real meaning. But prices may fluctuate in nonuniform ways, dependent not only on local labour market conditions, but also on factors affecting national or international trade. Furthermore, in order to look at wages over time, historians necessarily focus on regular and formulaic sources that are easily comparable – seigneurial accounts of cash expenditure, for example. But this ignores irregular records of nonmonetary elements, such as gifts; and, indeed, there is some evidence to suggest that in

England, while cash wages were to some degree kept down in accord with the Statute of Labourers of 1351, landowners found ways of circumventing the legislation (to which they themselves were subject) by providing an additional 'wage' in gifts. In other words, a potentially important part of the economic transaction was invisible to serial analysis of cash wages.[18] A graph or chart or set of statistics is only as good as the evidence from which it is drawn; and that evidence will always have some lacunae, and on occasion may be completely misleading.

To turn now to the other aspect of economics, the fragmentary nature of medieval evidence has made it difficult for historians to use economic theory in regard to the period with any confidence. Analyses of medieval economics have tended to be either extremely micro – the fortunes of a particular monastic estate – or hugely macro – the great patterns of international trade over a long period of time. In each case, what we don't know raises doubts over what is presented; a point that could, of course, be made with regard to every area of history, but to which economic history is particular susceptible, due to its attempt to perceive the workings of systems in their entirety. Simple economic theory posits, for example, that a fall in population (as occurred in the later fourteenth century) should lead to a fall in land value, that this in turn leads to a fall in prices, and at the same time there should be a rise in wages. However, as the great economic historian M. M. Postan pointed out, human behaviour complicates the matter: wage earners were more likely to be attracted into tenant farming if rents were low, and hence they may disappear (as wage earners, at any rate) from the records. A study of wages may not therefore accurately reflect population levels. And, as already noted, there is a grey area around the notion of 'wage': the records usually allow one to study cash wages, which were certainly a major feature of later medieval society. But other benefits from an employer may have affected the attractiveness or otherwise of an apparent cash wage: not only gifts, payment in kind and barter, but also the provision of food and shelter, and the possibility of connecting oneself politically and socially, as well as economically, to a useful future benefactor such as a large monastery.

This is not to say that economic analysis is not possible –

a string of articles on late medieval England in the journal *Economic History Review* (itself founded by medievalists) attests otherwise – but that while modern economic theory can prompt certain questions, it is less likely that the levers of its conceptual machinery will provide a solid answer. A particular feature of medieval economic life was that, in some respects, its markets (in the broad sense of the word) worked differently from modern ones. It was not the case, as various historians have shown, that medieval economies were utterly pre-capitalist and paternalist: the apparent division and control of labour by guilds was frequently more an aspiration than a fact, and where it was at its strongest – in the production of wool and cloth in north Italian cities for example – it was part of a pre-modern economy closest to nineteenth- and twentieth-century industrialized capitalism, based on a large wage labour force often in tension with a small entrepreneurial elite.[19] Nor was the Church's prohibition against usury (lending at interest) quite the disbarment that one might expect: moneylending was common to all cities, and was far from limited to Jewish bankers. In the city of Bruges, a lack of supply of coinage in the fourteenth century meant that much business depended upon loans, and the use of letters of exchange and book transfers – aspects of modern, cashless banking. 'Usury' was defined here as lending at a rate greater than 2p in the pound per week – an annual rate of 43.3 per cent.[20] So parts of medieval society, particularly in the large cities and particularly from the thirteenth century onwards, had economic aspects not dissimilar to those of much later ages. But in other respects, medieval cultural expectations about profit, social roles, fair prices, and so forth mean that straightforward application of economic 'laws' of supply and demand, or 'rational choice theory', are extremely problematic. Take the staple of bread, often used as a key indicator of price fluctuations and standards of living. Local authorities set various requirements for bread, in weight, content and price, which meant that it did not operate as a normal good within a free market. These regulations had unexpected effects on the profit margins of medieval bakers, making particular kinds of loaves more profitable at certain times and less profitable at others. Bakers were all independent artisans, but they were not permitted to be entrepreneurs in the sense that, say, a cloth merchant might be. They were servants of the broader community, the common good, and the regulations sought to allow them a 'fair' income, rather than something governed by the ebb and flow of the market.[21]

Marxist perspectives, inasmuch as they are versions of economic theory, have provided two particular elements to medieval history. The first – shared by pretty much every historian of every period of every political stripe – is the insight that people's material circumstances tend to affect their social and cultural productions. Not many medieval historians nowadays then go on to talk about 'class' in a classically Marxist fashion, as coherent groups bound together (whether wittingly or otherwise) by their economic interests.[22] But a looser sense of class has pertained, and is in some areas making something of a comeback. Again, the theory at least prompts one to ask the question, 'Are the differential material circumstances of people in this part of medieval society affecting their ideas, expectations, perceptions, solidarities?' – whether or not one feels it can provide the whole answer. The other aspect of Marxism that pertains is the epic 'transition from feudalism to capitalism'. The stark and crude division of the span of western history into feudal and then capitalist societies does not much appeal to most medieval historians, partly because we tend to favour nuance over grand narratives, and partly because, for reasons discussed above regarding Bruges, it does not well represent the complex breadth of medieval experience. However, it is true that medieval economies and societies in aggregate are of a rather different kind to modern, capitalist societies; and the question of how, through what processes and on what timescale that change came about continues to be a topic of interest. Recent work suggests that some elements of capitalist 'modernity' – substantial wage labour and a market-based economy – need to be pushed well back into our period.[23] And, as we shall see in Chapter 4, the recent historiographical turn towards 'the global', particularly with regards to the flow of material resources and trade, also has an important medieval element.

Archaeology, Science and Material Culture

The image on the cover of this book reproduces a remarkable medieval object: an early thirteenth-century reliquary casket depicting the martyrdom of St Thomas Becket, now held in the Louvre in Paris. It is not particularly big – just under 17cm long, 13cm high, 6cm wide, not that much larger (other than in width) than the book you are holding – but its vibrant colours and design are, clearly, eye-catching. The stunning blue is enamel, that is, glass dust melted onto burnished copper. It is possible – though in fact not tremendously likely – that it once held a contact relic from the saint, perhaps a piece of blood-soaked clothing. It was undoubtedly an object for worship, more than simply artistic admiration. Often, when we say that an object from the distant past is 'remarkable', it is because of its rarity. In this case, what is remarkable is rather the opposite: it is but one among a really quite large number of very similar reliquaries depicting Becket's martyrdom, forty-five of which still survive today, all produced in the French city of Limoges between the late twelfth and early thirteenth century. Limoges in that period became famed for its enamel work, attracting commissions, and being sent as gifts, from as far afield as Uppsala, Rome and the crusader kingdoms of the Middle East. The Becket caskets vary in their precise details, but are almost all variants on the same design.

We might approach the casket as art historians, considering the design, its iconography, its stylistic relationship to other visual productions of this and other periods. We can think about it in relation to other reliquaries and saints' cults, as a focal point for worship. But we can also think about it as a material object, and in so doing open up further questions about how to treat 'things' as much as texts from our period. There are interesting questions, as yet not fully answered, about the raw materials that went into its production, and into the production of many other enamelled items from the same place.[24] For example, Limoges did not itself produce copper, and it appears that the metal was imported there from several different sites elsewhere. The powdered glass from which the enamel was produced was not made in the same way as that used in contemporary stained-glass windows; indeed, there is reason to think that some of the powder may have come from re-using ancient Roman glass tesserae, though in such volume that either they were being imported from Italy or else someone in southwest France had worked out how to produce a similar kind of glass. One of the underlying substances in the admixture for the glass is 'natron', a form of soda ash found naturally in Egypt. Was this imported to Limoges? Or was another source found locally, though no longer apparent to us today? We can ask how Limoges enamel became so popular and widespread, noting in partial answer that the city sat on major trade and pilgrimage routes. And we can think about how the embodied human experience of interacting with this particular Limoges casket might vary between a certain ritual familiarity for its ecclesiastical guardians, a wider laity, most of whom might at best occasionally glimpse it at a distance, and the physical knowledge of its producers, those whose fingers knew the coolness of copper and the heat of melting glass, and who might view any such object in morphological relation to the many other variant forms produced in much the same time and place.

As mentioned in Chapter 1, the general consensus among historians today is that medieval people were more literate, and much more familiar with documentary culture, than older stereotypes of the 'Dark Ages' would suggest. Nonetheless, it is also true that, for the vast majority of medieval people, listening to a text being read was, if not quite 'rare', then something reserved to particular and limited occasions; and being involved in the creation of a text was an even more specific and unusual action. People throughout the middle ages spent most of their time not reading or writing, but doing things that we all still do – eating, excreting, sleeping, tidying and cleaning their domestic space, buying and selling or bartering things – and some things that only a few of us now do: agricultural labour, animal husbandry, brewing beer, going on pilgrimage, and so forth. All these things have left some trace in the documentary record, but the written sources only ever capture a snapshot moment, and necessarily miss out the vast majority of human experience. For earlier periods – the fall of the Roman Empire up till, let us say, 1100 – few kinds of document exist to tell us much about such activities, and almost none that recount them for other than the social elite.

However, what does survive is material culture. Some of it, like the Becket casket, is the product of international flows of human activity; other elements bear the fuzzy imprint of daily life in a way that texts do not. All of it can tell us things about the middle ages that writing does not record.

Archaeologists work with things and places rather than texts, and their sense of how to 'read' such materials differs in important aspects from those of historians. There has indeed been a degree of tension between the two disciplines, usually implicit on the historians' side, but more explicit on the other. Archaeology, partly because of the techniques it utilizes and partly through disciplinary choice, tends to see itself as a more 'scientific' subject than history. All kinds of science – biology, DNA analysis, carbon dating, computer modelling, magnetic imaging and the like – are used in the service of archaeology (certain of those sciences were fundamental to researchers' ability to understand the chemical composition of the materials in Limoges enamel, for example). Its sense of how to investigate a historical theme, and its framework and purposes of investigation, tend to differ from those of historians. The root cause of the disciplinary tensions was historians' past tendency to treat archaeology as 'the handmaid of history' – a useful helper, but incapable of independent insight – which led some earlier archaeologists to declare the independence of the spade, and to claim an objective trustworthiness for the archaeological record, in comparison to all those 'biased' texts beloved by historians. Such polarized viewpoints are today more rare, though some disjunctures remain.[25]

Partly because of these differences, but also because of the innate gap between the material and textual records, the findings of historians and archaeologists can, however, differ markedly, even when treating the very same subject. For example, studies of castles in England by historians, working on the basis of documentary sources, for a long time proposed that castle-building, on the classic motte-and-bailey pattern, was brought to the country by the Normans after the Conquest in 1066. They were defensive structures, part of the process by which a military elite subjugated the native population. Archaeological surveys, however, pointed out that motte-and-bailey castles do not seem to be present in Normandy itself prior to 1066: the Normans thus could not have 'brought them over', and must at best have invented them during the process of conquest. However, the archaeologists have argued, excavation of pre-Conquest sites in England may demonstrate the prior existence of large, circular defensive structures, much like the surviving castles. Castles – depending on how one defines the term – could be more indigenous than one might think.[26] Furthermore, more recent, interdisciplinary work has argued that the siting and style of castles was very rarely a matter purely of military and defensive capability: they are better understood as structures that communicate lordship – social and political dominance – through symbolic, as much as practical, means.[27] What look reassuringly 'solid' and objective – large stone structures plonked firmly in the landscape – can in fact turn out to be as prey to interpretative complexity as the most ephemeral work of fiction.

It is, of course, not always the case that text and material remains prompt radically opposing interpretations. The best work combines insights from both perspectives, as in the exciting recent discovery of traces of the precious blue stone lapis lazuli in the tooth tartar of a medieval woman buried at a monastic site in Dalheim, Germany, probably in the twelfth century. The microscopic analysis and identification of the mineral fragments have been combined with the existing textual work on German nuns as scribes, to suggest quite convincingly that the traces of the mineral indicate the woman's role as a producer of illuminated manuscripts.[28] More normally, the two disciplines complement rather than contradict each other. This has very much been the case in the history and buildings archaeology of late medieval civic life, analyses of medieval monasticism and its culture, or, to take an area of particular current interest, the study of death. Late medieval culture produced a particular genre of writing on death – the *ars moriendi*, or art of dying well – that focused on the theological aspects of sin and salvation; and, as in most cultures, death had been a theme in medieval literature of all kinds for centuries. Thus, the written evidence, in broad terms, points research towards beliefs about death and the afterlife, the desire for salvation and the fear of damnation, and is generally directed 'beyond' this world. Study of the material culture of death – mortuary practices, funerary monuments, grave-goods and the like – adds a different perspective over a longer time frame.[29] While supernatural beliefs obviously continue to have importance, other more social aspects are brought into view. Thus the siting of burials can be read for evidence of social stratification, and grave-goods (the various precious or peculiar objects interred with the deceased) can help us interpret social display and funerary culture.

The combination of history and archaeology has produced a sophisticated analysis of the cultures of death for different periods, and more broadly the complex ways in which the surviving material evidence may be interpreted for markers of cultural identity. For the early middle ages, differences in mortuary practices were long used as badges of different ethnic identities: by looking at how people buried their dead, archaeologists attempted to identify to which religious and ethnic groups they belonged. However, recent work has pointed out problems with this, noting for example that from English evidence there is no clear division between unadorned (notionally 'Christian') burials and those containing substantial grave-goods ('pagan'); rather, there is a blurred continuum, with a suspicion that grave-goods came and went in waves, affected by economic and cultural factors.[30] Through the use of both textual and archaeological sources, Bonnie Effros has argued that Merovingian funerary ritual employed elements of Germanic and Roman traditions, so diagnosing a 'pure' ethnic identity is therefore not possible. Where variations in funerary practice are found within cemeteries, one should not assume that ethnicity is the only factor: age, gender and social status may also have affected the ritual elements of a particular burial. And, Effros suggests, funerals are symbolically rich, ideological acts; they do not simply 'reflect' an ethnic identity, but can produce and transform it.[31] In a similar fashion, a very careful analysis of treasure hoards and grave-goods (among other matters) in the sixth- and seventh-century Danube region has complicated previous ascriptions of 'barbarian' and 'Slavic' ethnic groupings. Earlier work, for example, noted differences in brooch design between two areas, and, from this and other evidence, diagnosed the existence of two particular barbarian communities, Lombard and Gepid. However, it has been pointed out that the different styles can be found elsewhere in Europe; and other styles can be found within apparently Lombard and Gepid 'regions'. Similar arguments can be advanced for the alleged 'incomer' group, the Slavs. In fact, argues Florin Curta, rather than imagining 'a great flood of Slavs coming out of the Pripet marshes' to bang up against the edge of the last of the Roman Empire, one might better see 'Slav' identity as something formed within existing communities, in response to the vast building programme initiated by the emperor Justinian on the Danube frontier and in the Balkans.[32]

In this and other areas, particularly for the early middle ages, the richness of archaeological material far surpasses that of the extant texts, and may make us aware of things otherwise completely unsuspected. Some elements of late medieval culture are seen only through objects and never mentioned in texts: a number of remarkable pilgrim badges depicting male and female genitalia have been found in Germany, the Netherlands and elsewhere. These cheap, plebeian objects have no known textual glosses, and we would have no hint of the curious mixture of sacred and profane found here, were it not for the material survivals. They remain open to interpretation.[33] Landscape archaeology can indicate the possibility of deep-seated patterns to human culture and politics: the study of settlement patterns, for example, can be mapped in different ways to agricultural practice, and in turn to soil type. Careful analysis of different kinds of soil, and the necessary demands of making it agriculturally productive, suggest that the very ground upon which we stand may influence all kinds of cultural complexities. For example, a certain clay soil that must be ploughed very swiftly necessitates agricultural collaboration, which leads to closely nucleated settlement patterns, which in turn facilitate collaborative action in more complex areas, and perhaps shape certain kinds of social and political identities.[34]

Archaeological study has also had a great impact on the study of the medieval economy. Take Scandinavia, for which very little written evidence exists prior to 1200. Analysis of physical objects and their movements, however, suggests the existence of some important trading links over very considerable distances: whetstones found hundreds of miles from their source, Norwegian iron discovered in Denmark, and so forth. Coin finds at Scandinavian churches also suggest that – as was the case in other, better-documented, parts of Europe – they probably served as venues for markets.[35] Archaeology has in fact substantially altered our understanding of the early medieval economy. For a long time, the debate was framed by a thesis developed by the Belgian scholar Henri Pirenne (1862–1935).[36] Pirenne argued that the rise of an Islamic empire in the seventh century severed the long-distance trading routes of the late antique period, collapsing the early medieval economy from one based on intercity trade across the Mediterranean to one landlocked and limited to agrarian simplicity. However, more recent archaeological work has considerably revised this picture. Numismatics (the study of coins) permits one to trace trade exchange of at least certain kinds: if Arabic coinage from the eighth and ninth centuries is found in southern France and northern Spain, and eighth-century Byzantine coins in Marseille, then a picture of grand-scale trading links begins to emerge. The movement of certain kinds of prestige pottery (locatable by identifying its kiln or, for later finds, the type of clay used) strongly implies the movement of other kinds of more perishable goods, such as silk, alongside it. Recently, the field of bioarchaeology has been able to examine trace elements in human skeletal remains, indicating diet and the presence of nonlocal, and hence traded, foodstuffs. Archaeological survivals of various kinds have suggested the existence of early medieval trading places – markets, one assumes – well beyond the famous (and usually coastal) emporia; thus, what were previously thought of as inactive backwaters seem to have played a larger role in the economy. The most recent grand synthesis of the material across the early middle ages has essentially reversed Pirenne's model, arguing that it was precisely the presence of new markets in North Africa and the Middle East that underpinned the growth of the European economy.[37] Thus archaeological insights can completely revise the historical record.

These are examples of where material evidence, and specific archaeological study, have complemented and surpassed text-based history's viewpoint. But archaeology has played another important role: encouraging medieval historians to think, and think differently, about aspects of their study that they tend to take for granted. One is the importance of reflecting on texts as physical objects in themselves. Part of this has older roots in manuscript codicology – the study of how manuscripts are put together – but text-as-material-culture brings further insights. One can think about texts as objects in relationship to other, nontextual, objects: a book of hours, for example, can be studied with regard to not only prayers and liturgical writing, but also other devotional objects such as statues, altar pieces and miniatures, and moreover as a part of what one might call 'domestic treasure' – the various precious objects that are valued both materially and for the sense of status they impart, and that tend to be distributed within kin groups via wills and so forth. Historians usually think first about what a manuscript says; archaeologists encourage us to think about what one does with a manuscript, which may include many other activities than simply reading it. Recent developments in non-invasive sampling techniques have also opened up further elements in the 'material' aspect of manuscripts, allowing collaboration between archaeologists and codicologists to identify not only the kind of animal skin used in the production of parchment, but where the skin of the same beast ended up in multiple manuscripts, which may well therefore be linked in terms of production. Identification of the type of animal skin facilitates analysis of aspects of the environment within which those animals once lived, including, for example, diseases suffered by the animals. And there is some possibility – though not without considerable complications regarding interpretation – of recovering the DNA of the human users of manuscripts.[38]

Another aspect that archaeologists (in concert with anthropologists) have brought to historical attention is the study of space. There are various particular skills that archaeology provides here, from highly technical issues regarding comparative dating and excavation techniques, the use of aerial photography and electronic mapping, to the more basic but essential ability to construct a meaningful topography of an area. For example, a study of non-ecclesiastical and nonpalatial structures in medieval Constantinople (modern Istanbul) uses various sources, including texts, to build an initial picture of the possible aspects of civic layout: the variety of possible building types, and a sense of different 'residential zones' (monumental, coastal, high- and low-status residential, and open land). A very careful and comparative analysis of the building remains and archaeological excavations then permits some working hypotheses about the location, design and extent of domestic and commercial buildings, and an idea of street layouts.[39] Late medieval cities sometimes provide the textual sources to reconstruct topographies, but archaeological surveys are essential and, for much of our period, the only option.

Having provided some tools for mapping space, archaeology also encourages us to think about it in different ways. First, change over time. Continuities and contrasts in building techniques and styles can help here, and the presence of new material features at different moments in time points to the changing usage of buildings and spaces. Thus the study of Constantinople mentioned above suggests that some late antique elite residential buildings were converted into churches during the early medieval period. Second, and perhaps most influentially on recent medieval history, both archaeology and anthropology encourage reflection on the social uses and meanings of space. Archaeological theory thinks of material culture and space as part of ongoing human processes – in movement, rather than static, and enmeshed within shifting (and sometimes competing) ideas of society, politics and culture. Roberta Gilchrist's influential study of English nunneries has suggested various ways in which architecture and space were implicated in social and gender distinctions. Features such as moats and courtyards, found in various East Anglian foundations, had more in common with manorial settlements than with other monastic topographies, and indicate close connections between the nuns and the lesser gentry. By drawing access maps (abstracted plans of the available routes through a building), Gilchrist demonstrates that male monasteries were considerably more 'permeable' than nunneries: an outsider could more easily get into and move between a variety of monastic rooms, whereas various parts of nunneries were only accessible through limited and extended routes. Women's enclosure was thereby more physically guaranteed than men's. Thus monastic space is fashioned not only through practical necessity, but also through issues of ideology, power and gender.[40] Recent historical work on space has further emphasized its shifting and contested nature. The English marketplace has been analysed as a site of both horizontal social interaction through trade and gossip, and vertical expressions of power through the enaction of public penances and the display of executed criminals; the locations and social meanings of prostitution in late medieval Prague have been read as being transformed under the influence of different religious ideals.[41] These studies, and others like them, engage most directly with anthropology; but it is largely to archaeology that medieval history owes the original inspiration for discussion of the physical world and its meanings.[42]

I mentioned above how recent developments in scientific techniques have opened up new potentials in the study of medieval manuscripts. This is in fact but one specific example of how archaeologists and historians, in collaboration with the other natural sciences, have been leaping ahead in terms of technical possibilities. Two general areas have probably been the most transformative, and continue to proffer considerable new possibilities for debate. One is the analysis of DNA, the other the study of climatic variation (principally but not solely via dendrochronology). In recent years it has become much faster, and relatively less costly, to analyse DNA, and there have been very clever technical developments over how to extract it from surviving remains. As already noted above, there is a wide variety of possibilities for DNA analysis; perhaps the most extensive thus far have been the study of disease, and the analysis of early medieval migration. For the former, the most important discovery, bringing decades of debate more or less to an end, has been the identification of *Yersinia pestis* as the disease pathogen responsible for the Black Death. While the initial discovery was challenged by some, follow-up studies have refined techniques and confirmed the identification, most recently sequencing the whole genome of *Y. pestis*.[43] Studies of the late antique Justinianic plague also identify *Y. pestis* and have recently demonstrated how the DNA from that outbreak forms a novel strain of the disease, potentially providing more broadly an explanation for why some historical accounts of past plagues describe transmission or symptoms that differ from those expected from modern experience.[44] As importantly, however, the scientific discoveries here have further opened out the debate rather than bringing it to a close; current discussion, assisted by ongoing genetic analysis, is grappling with the likely geographical origin and spread of the fourteenth-century plague, and the complex interplay of social, political, climatic and zoological factors that caused it to spread.[45]

With regard to early medieval migration, scholars have been revisiting areas of debate noted above regarding the movement of 'barbarian' peoples. A large project, led by Patrick Geary, has been using various means of analysis, but focused centrally on sequencing medieval DNA recovered from multiple burial sites, to reconsider the case for 'Lombard' (or 'Longobard') migration in the later sixth century. The evidence does strongly suggest the movement of peoples from what is now Hungary into northern Italy, and genetic intermingling thereafter.[46] Science in this sense is majorly supplementing what are otherwise rather sparse and rhetorically inflected written sources recounting 'the Lombard invasion'. As Geary and others note, however, the science does not simply explain the history, nor do the haplogroup (= genetic group sharing a common ancestor) identifications equate simply to an 'ethnic' identity, still less a political one. In these and similar areas, medievalists must be extremely diligent in fighting off any collapse back into a nineteenth-century set of essentialist notions about 'race', in order to avoid feeding current public misconceptions (and political appropriation by the racist Far Right).[47]

To turn now to climate: there are various means by which climate scientists attempt to establish the very long history of climate variation – ice core samples, tree rings, oceanic sediment – a general purpose being of course to establish beyond all doubt that the modern production of carbon emissions has brought us into an unprecedented period of anthropogenic climate crisis. The middle ages have been particularly implicated in past debates over climate change, because of what appears to be a 'medieval warm period' or 'medieval climate anomaly' from *c*.950 to 1250 CE, when temperatures in Europe were generally higher than in later periods, up until the last decades of the twentieth century. (Studies continue to support a 'medieval warm period', but have clarified that the rate of recent climate change is considerably greater than in the past. They also strongly suggest that medieval warmth was largely the outcome of reduced volcanic activity and increased solar output, and note regional temperature fluctuations during the period.)[48] Recent work in dendrochronology – the examination of tree-ring growth that can potentially map year-by-year environmental changes – is starting to provide the potential for a closer link between historical and scientific analysis, to move beyond establishing the fact of climate variation to analyse past human reactions to it. This is in part because dendrochronology can map, fairly robustly (albeit for a specific region), individual years and climate events such as volcanic eruptions; and because the science is now as interested in regional and seasonal variations within the climate record as it is in the overall aggregate picture. Given local and time-specific data, it is thus possible to correlate attested disasters – such as specific years (1161, 1230) of crop failure and subsequent famine in medieval Novgorod – to anomalously cold years, potentially providing confirmation of chronicle reports.

There is great potential here for medieval historians, and some have already turned to climate shifts – particularly the move, in the early fourteenth century, from the medieval warm period into a much cooler and wetter environment in northern Europe – as a major element (along with disease) in creating a fundamental transition in agriculture, society and economy in the later middle ages.[49] The overall trend was to a cooler climate, but the specific effect in, for example, late medieval England was to create extremes of weather patterns, varying unpredictably between years, hugely disruptive to agricultural production and probably interlocking with the intermittent spread of plague to cause further suffering.[50] On occasion, climate scientists are tempted to suggest that temperature and rainfall fluctuations might *explain* certain events, such as the unexpected withdrawal of the Mongols from Hungary in 1242 (in the face of a sudden shift to major rainfall and cooling in that region).[51] However, while some written sources, such as late medieval serial records of crop harvests, can provide a reasonably robust data set to compare with climate evidence, for the largely narrative sources of earlier times we may wish to preserve the cultural situatedness of our written material; when early medieval writers note dramatic environmental events such as floods or storms, they could have been reacting to objective external events, but were primarily casting their world in the rhetoric of biblical punishment and warning.[52]

So the advances in science present challenges for us also, not least in how to work collaboratively with people from truly different disciplines. For most medieval historians, myself included, 'reading into' a subject like dendrochronology or DNA analysis is much more challenging than if one were attempting to grapple with recent anthropology or social science. The key issue – a point that I owe to conversation with the dendrochronologist Ulf Büntgen – is that it is rarely possible to become 'fully expert' in a totally different discipline. What is needed, rather, is the desire to foster open dialogue between disciplines, including the willingness on all sides to admit to uncertainty, gaps in the data, and current methodological weakness. With regard to climate, debate over the fact of the current climate crisis is essentially concluded (other than for the most stubbornly deluded); how historians, and particularly medieval historians, can now contribute is via collaborative discussion of the ways in which human societies interact with, and react to, shifts in climate and other environmental factors. The sciences, at the cutting edge of one kind of 'materiality', present tremendous opportunities; but medievalist and other historians are best served if we treat them as partners in an ongoing discussion, neither as masters nor handmaidens to our work.

Texts and Cultural Theory

Its claws have driven through the cloud, it climbs up with so
   great a strength,
I see it grays so like the day, it will unshroud the day which
   will then take at length
his lady from this noble man, for whom I won a difficult
   entry.
I will bring him forth from here if I can: his many virtues
   demand no less of me.[53]

The words are those of a watchman, servant to a lady, prompted by the dawning light to consider waking her and her knightly lover, and bid him leave her bed. They form the opening stanza of a short poem written in the early thirteenth century by Wolfram von Eschenbach, himself a knight and author also of *Parzival*, one of the greatest of medieval Arthurian romances. Such a text has an obvious importance to literary critics, interested in the development and technical analysis of literature; but I want to consider here how one approaches such a piece as a historian – and, more broadly, to explore ways in which historians adopt certain tools from literary analysis.

As with archaeology, there is a close relation between the study of history and literature. Both deal primarily with written texts (though in the case of Wolfram's work, texts almost certainly experienced in oral performance, and possibly also composed that way), both are used to close and careful reading of their materials in order to extract all possible meaning, and both are interested in how one moves from a specific text to the wider world of the period. The disciplines have again had a tendency to squabble. Literary scholars have sometimes been prone to appropriating simplistic histories as context for their textual analyses, while simultaneously decrying historians' lack of analytical sophistication. Historians tend towards knee-jerk suspicions about abstract theorizing, and have on occasion read literary texts in a lumpenly literal fashion. Medieval literary texts were conscious of their own literariness, playing with stylistic conventions of great subtlety, alluding to themes not immediately obvious to a modern reader, and were usually soaked in waves of potential meaning rather than claiming any direct referentiality to life. But this does not mean that historians cannot make any use of them. Some narrative poems do contain information on deeds and events: it would be difficult to write the history of the Albigensian Crusade (1209–29) without the *Chanson de la Croisade* for example, and Scandinavian sagas have been vital, albeit hotly contested, evidence for Iceland and Norway.

But more importantly, literature (and indeed other notionally 'historical' sources) can be read for attitudes, ideas, patterns of thinking and the like. Wolfram's poem tells us nothing of real events, but it can show us something about cultural mores. The watchman has both a loyalty to his lady, and an admiration for the knight with whom she sleeps; there is tension between her desire for her lover and her honour; and, as the sun rises to announce the day, the space of the lady's chamber is slowly shifting from a private realm to a potentially public arena. The poem strongly hints that the lady has a husband whom the knight is cuckolding. One need not assume that the poet and the audience approve of or aspire to this situation (although it did of course sometimes occur); what is important is that it dramatizes a set of tensions between individual desires of all kinds, and the demands of community and allegiance. Such a tension is familiar in other literature of the period, such as the love affair between Lancelot and Arthur's queen Guinevere. All this would make sense to Wolfram's audience, both emotionally and intellectually – and hence it gives an insight into the shape of their thought and feelings.

Perhaps most interesting is the theme of gender, not only the lady's femininity but the knight's (and watchman's) masculinity. Later in the poem, it is clear that it is also the knight's honour that is at stake, and in the stanza quoted above the watchman says that his own duty is prompted by the knight's very many virtues (*sîn vil manigiu tugent*). Masculinity would here appear to be something public, affective and demanding, and about relations between men and other men as much as between men and women. In the idealization of the poem, it also differs by class: the knight can find masculine fulfilment in his lady love sexually, while the watchman must be happy with rendering service, a different kind of manliness. This pattern is found not only in 'chivalric' situations, but in other areas also, such as artisanal crafts and university intellectuals.[54] Thus, while a literary text may not often provide 'fact', it can tell us about ways of talking and writing and hence thinking.

Literary theory has prompted historians to recognize the importance of language more widely, not only in realms of literature but in all written sources. Language does not simply reflect the world around us; it mediates that world, in both directions, in that our experience of the world is framed and interpreted by language (or, more broadly, cultural ideas and practices), and in turn we attempt to shape the world, and other people's experiences of it, by using language (culture) to present ideas of how we think it is or should be. A good realm of examples can be found in the language of politics. The ways in which elites explain and justify unequal and hierarchical power structures – the hierarchical but reciprocal 'body politic' for example, found in John of Salisbury's twelfth-century *Policraticus* and in many later texts and images – are not simply 'reflections' of the political realm, nor even of how people thought about it. They are, rather, attempts to shape both the thoughts and the reality, and (in this particular image) to make a particular distribution of power and authority appear natural and hence beyond question. Following the work of Quentin Skinner and John Pocock for later periods, historians of medieval politics have begun to think about vocabularies of power, tracing for example the complex and shifting meanings ascribed to the term 'the commons' in later medieval England.[55] Mark Ormrod has invited historians of that period to think about the complexities of the basic language itself – the slow and intermittent shift from Latin and French to English in the language of royal government – partly in terms of political constructions of national identity but also in relation to fears of vernacular sedition and heresy, and a series of specific negotiations between king and parliament.[56]

It is worth noting, in regard to the last two examples, that what has been termed 'the linguistic turn' incorporates various different ways in which historians have become interested in language. Vocabularies, rhetorics and the meanings of 'keywords' are one area; the politics of vernacularization, together with the link between native language and identity, is another. A third area would be consideration of textual form and its cultural contexts. Literary texts can very obviously have certain formal characteristics, in terms of rhyme-schemes, rhythm, themes, and so forth. They carry meaning partly through these embedded structures. But what we think of as 'historical' texts can in some ways be viewed similarly. Historians have long noted the formulaic nature of various records – indeed, this has always been a part of 'diplomatic' (the study of documents, diploma in Latin). But literary analysis can encourage an appreciation of records' structural similarities that go beyond the more obvious repetitions. Many sources contain narrative, little works of fiction that mould real events into convenient shapes. Preaching *exempla* are an obvious example, and by looking at an array of such materials, an historian can discern some common structural patterns they share. *Exempla* usually have a four-part structure comprising a setting, a test, success or failure, and damnation or salvation. Stories extolling male clerical chastity tend to fall into a limited number of narrative patterns of self-control or divine intervention, shaped by the slightly conflicting themes of the miraculous and masculine self-governance.[57] Narrative can be found also in less obvious places, such as trial documents (as discussed in Chapter 2). Deponents and judges each bring something to the record: the former attempt to persuade the court of something (their innocence, their victimhood, their ignorance), while the latter provide a juridical grid of interpretation and categorization. These, in combination with the textual habits of the recording scribes, produce the stories presented in trial records, and such narratives bear the imprint of wider cultural expectations – sometimes differing expectations.[58] Thus an appreciation of the narrative elements in our sources can help us, not by attempting to divide the 'true' from the 'false', but by pointing to the wider framework of images, ideas and assumptions within which someone attempted to have their story accepted as true.

Language, narrative, storytelling are all social, embedded in and shaping the world around them, and hence important to the historian as well as the literary critic. Language is not simply a means of communication; it is a social deed. As Michael Toch puts it: 'By the very act of speaking, people act and are acted upon.' He goes on to illustrate the point by exploring verbal encounters between lords and peasants in the world of Wolfram von Eschenbach, high medieval Germany. Some documentary accounts, Toch demonstrates, mimic literary encounters in displaying vast disparities of status and power between lord and serf, the latter no more than a tool of the former. But by the thirteenth century a different kind of speech can be found, the peasantry talking in a collective voice as a legitimate group, capable of negotiation with their lords.[59] There has been substantial work in recent times on medieval towns and cities that looks beyond abstract treatises to the evidence of contemporary cultural productions – such as poems, songs and plays produced in the late medieval Low Countries, or the quotidian documents produced by civic governmental processes – to analyse competing political 'voices', addressing ideas of 'citizenship', governance and justice from a broader perspective.[60]

One of the insights literary and cultural theory has provided to medieval historians is the degree to which social experience is shaped by language – or, more broadly, cultural expressions structured like languages, such as the regulation of clothing and appearance, the conduct of public rituals, and so forth. An area of particular interest has been gender. Feminist medievalists have long analysed the differential experience of men and women, looking first and foremost to socioeconomic conditions for the low status of female labour, the structure of the household and family and the effects that lifecycle had on women's power. Pioneers in this field also pointed to the power of ecclesiastical misogyny, and this cultural element has in recent years come to the fore, with added complexity. Theorists point out how unstable language is: a structure, but one untethered to fixed points of reference, and hence prey to shifting meanings and innate tensions. Gender, as a system of relations between people and as a constituent factor in people's self-identity, is thus argued to be less solid and stable than one might assume. It is not simply the case that there are men and there are women, based on a set of bodily differences, from which a certain set of behaviours arises. The medieval period is a particularly interesting field in which to explore the complexities of gender, because of the way in which other social classifications cut across the binary division of man/woman. Scandinavian sagas, Carol Clover suggests, present one unitary model of dominance and power – what we might assume to be 'masculinity' – but in fact are open to both men and women, if they are sufficiently extraordinary. The late medieval clergy in northern Europe, on the other hand, could be seen as a kind of 'third gender', being denied access to traditionally masculine modes of achieving adulthood (marriage, being head of household, etc.) while, by definition, not being feminine.[61]

In these and other areas, cultural theory has encouraged historians to look again at what they assume is 'natural' or taken for granted. A principal aspect has been to see all facets of personal identity as constructed rather than naturally arising. Indeed, the notion of individual identity has been historicized in studies of the middle ages. In what was essentially a dismissive move, the cultural historian Jakob Burckhardt (1818–97) claimed that the medieval period had no sense of individuality, and people always thought of themselves as members of groups; the shift to a more 'modern' notion of selfhood, he argued, came only with the Renaissance.[62] A pioneering generation of medievalists questioned the validity of this, primarily by moving the debate back to the twelfth century.[63] Subsequent work has questioned not only the chronology, but the terms of the debate: was an ahistorical abstract entity – 'the individual' – discovered, produced, brought into being in a fixed way at any point? Or is it rather that different kinds of identities – some individual, but in our period more collective – were produced in different circumstances? Thus Caroline Walker Bynum has pointed to the way in which pious self-identity depended on choosing between a variety of group identities in the twelfth century, and the importance of imitation as a way of literally remaking the self: as Hugh of St Victor (1096–1141) wrote of the example of the saints:

> We are imprinted by these things through imitations . . . But it should be known that unless wax is first softened, it does not receive the form, so indeed a man is not bent to the form of virtue through the power of another's action unless first through humility he is softened away from the hardness of all pride and contradiction.[64]

This 'softening' sounds very unlike modern conceptions of individuality; and Hugh's programme for achieving a pious identity clearly depends on the example of God and the assistance of 'another's action' – being part of a life that is to some extent regulated. Consideration of different kinds of identity and individuality, and the means of their construction, have continued to be the focus of attention. Recent work on chivalry has explored the ways in which the apparent tensions contained in that ideology – between violence and peacekeeping, between the individual knight errant and the Arthurian Round Table companionate model – may be seen as essential elements in producing identity, understood within a specifically medieval context.[65]

It is important to end this chapter with a return to reflection on the medievalness of this and other matters. I do not wish to state dogmatically that medieval people were essentially different from modern people, any more than I would want to assume the reverse. The question of sameness or difference – identification or alterity – is an important and continuing debate. A great strength of the kinds of theories touched upon here is that they help us to see that one can relinquish the desire for 'essence' and a single, unequivocal answer to such a question. Identity is contextual, and the experience of that identity fluctuates through the contours of age, class, social setting and the like. The kind of subaltern, submissive identity one might imagine for Wolfram von Eschenbach's watchman – an identity predicated on his subservience to lord and lady – need not be read as the limits of all possible identities such a man might possess. As we know from other evidence, someone of the watchman's class held a superior position to other secular men. If married, he might also enjoy a position of authority as head of his own household. As he aged, other offices could become open to him. And on occasion – as was the case quite frequently in fifteenth and early sixteenth-century Germany – servants, peasants and serfs gathered the collective strength to deny their subservient identity, and challenge their lords in open rebellion.[66]

4
Debating the Middle Ages

History is a collaborative enterprise – or, to put it another way, an ongoing argument. The argument is conducted, mostly, in polite terms of mutual academic respect, and what lies behind the argument is, usually, differences in evidence, viewpoint, perspective and insight. I have no ambition for this chapter to chart every contour of recent medievalist debate, as this would require a much bigger book. There are many specific areas of discussion, the importance of which have shifted at different points in time. A perennial favourite has been medieval demographic change, with particular attention to the depredations (or otherwise) of the Black Death of the mid-fourteenth century, estimates of which have varied between around 10 per cent and 70 per cent of any given population; current views seem to suggest something around 40 per cent, but emphasize the importance (culturally, politically and economically) of local variation – and, as Samuel Cohn has argued, the major return of plague in the 1360s was perhaps of greater long-term social and cultural impact than the initial onslaught.[1] Some topics were once heated but are now seen as rather outmoded – the effects (good or bad) of the Norman Conquest of England, for example – or have settled into a background consensus that yet awaits major new discussion – the general drift of the 'twelfth-century renaissance', for instance. Other debates grapple with terms largely now viewed as overly schematic, but which nonetheless continue to frame the area, such as whether medieval Iberian society was best characterized by *convivencia* (relatively peaceful coexistence between Christian, Jewish and Islamic populations) or *reconquista* (violent conflict as Christian rulers extended their dominion southwards).

Most specific areas of study have, at any given time, a particular interpretative dispute in progress, and it's worth trying to understand the wider historiographical contexts within which these specific arguments are conducted. For example, in an area I know well – medieval heresy – current discussions concern the degree to which heresies had independent existences or were the constructions of orthodox power.[2] This theme preoccupies scholars working on various areas from eleventh-century France to fifteenth-century England, in part because of the continued reverberations of a particular book – R. I. Moore's *The Formation of a Persecuting Society* (1985) – which made historians radically reappraise how they understood the relationship between heresy and orthodox authority.[3] But it is also a product of a wider historiographical tendency among many historians to focus on the ways in which our sources construct, rather than reflect, the reality around them. Arguments are thus shaped, in part, by the methodologies and ideologies immanent in the general business of doing history. Apart from really rather specific topics, usually concerned with the minutiae of high politics, it is rarely the case that debates or reappraisals are prompted solely by the discovery of previously unknown evidence. It is the case though that existing categories of source material are periodically seen afresh from a new perspective, or brought to bear on new areas – such as the use of canonization processes for writing social history, or the terse records of notarial practice for cultural histories of identity.[4]

In discussing here some debates within medieval history, I am therefore not claiming to present the most important topics for the field (for these will surely change), nor plotting all the ins and outs of particular areas (too specific a task), but attempting to indicate some general themes within which debates have been, and one suspects will be, conducted. Some historians would emphasize differences in the working methods, and means of debate, between early medieval and late medieval histories; it could be argued for example that the relatively sparse source material pre-1100 encourages more structural analyses and greater use of archaeological data, while later work has drawn more on large-scale serial analysis, and is more focused on those aspects of social history that are difficult to capture in earlier centuries. However, these differences are not absolute, and sometimes loom larger in the eye of the outside beholder than of the practitioner. I have therefore chosen to emphasize lines of analysis that have been – or could be – shared across the period as a whole.

Ritual

You were only a king if other people recognized you as a king. How one engineered recognition could vary: issuing laws and coinage, dispensing justice, building castles – or through violence. The royal status of Raoul, king of the West Franks, had not been acknowledged by Duke William of Auvergne, and so, in 924, the former raised an army against the latter and set off for Aquitaine. The forces met at the Loire, each camped on opposite sides of the river. Messengers passed back and forth all day in negotiation. An agreement was reached: William, on horseback, crossed the river, and then dismounted, to approach Raoul on foot. Raoul embraced William, and kissed him. The matter resolved, the two sides parted.[5]

What's in a kiss? How can such an embrace resolve weighty matters, apparently taking the place of pitched battle between warriors? At least part of the answer rests on the entire sequence of gestures: William crossed the river to Raoul (indicating submission); he did it on horseback (indicating status); he dismounted and approached on foot (indicating submission); Raoul embraced William (indicating status – but for both sides, as William did not adopt a more submissive pose, by kneeling for example); and Raoul bestowed a kiss (indicating status – and again, for both sides, treating William fraternally rather than demanding fealty). William had recognized Raoul's kingship – but Raoul was in fact prevented, then and thereafter, from crossing the Loire into the area of William's ducal authority. In the working out of these complexities we are dealing with a language of gestures, and witnessing the power and delicacy of ritual.

Rituals – whether loosely defined as symbolically meaning-ful action, or restricted to quasi-'scripted' formal activities – pervade medieval society, up and down the social strata. Royal courts were a constant dance of ritual movements: who sat where, who was positioned higher than whom, who passed what to whom, how a head was inclined, a hand turned, a gift rendered and a counter-gift returned. The lit-urgy was ritual, enacting daily the transformative miracle of the Eucharist, and (at least in the later middle ages) the no less miraculous production of communal accord through the kiss of peace, exchanged between neighbours at the conclusion of mass. Punishments from Church courts demanded ritual humiliations, usually being beaten around the church and the market while barefoot and partially unclad. From the twelfth century, if not earlier, towns and cities staged rituals of var-ious kinds: the theatre of royal entries to the town, more or less devout processions deployed in the case of deaths, cele-brations, saints' days, and calls for divine intervention, the various rituals of guild artisans and confraternity members. Villages undertook annual rituals of different kinds: leading a plough around a fire at the beginning of the year (in the hope of ensuring a good harvest), the sexually charged games of Hocktide (the women chasing and binding men on one day, the roles reversed the day after), the wild celebrations at Midsummer, the annual 'beating of the bounds' that marked the edge of the parish (the children smacked at each way-marker, to drum the geography into their memories).[6]

It is not only the middle ages, of course, that used ritual, and anthropologists enjoy pointing out to modern audiences the ritual behaviour that enters our own lives, such as foot-ball games, formal dinner parties, stag and hen nights, and so forth. But medievalists have a particular concern with ritual, because of the key role it appeared to play in three overlap-ping areas: the negotiation of political power, the sustenance of hegemonic Christianity, and the renewal of peace and com-munity. In each of these areas one sees ritual activities in oper-ation, sometimes alongside, but often in the stead of, other formalized or legalistic structures. While one suspects that modern life would continue fairly smoothly without football matches, dinner parties or outlets of routine bacchanalia, it is tremendously difficult to imagine how medieval politics and society could have been conducted in the absence of kisses, embraces, prostrations, tears and the other elements of ritual language.

Ritual has thus been of particular interest to historians of early medieval politics (with some recent interest in later periods also), religion and society, and late medieval civic culture. Their specific concerns do not always coincide, and discussions have tended to run along slightly different lines in each area. Work on early medieval politics has been guided in large part by the available narrative sources, which give a clear emphasis to ritual forms of behaviour in the settlement of disputes (such as between William and Raoul), and which seem to suggest that ritual behaviour formed an essential part of what a later age would call diplomacy, while being an intriguingly 'unwritten' code; the 'rules of the game' as Gerd Althoff has described it.[7] Study in this area has largely tried to understand how ritual fitted into other forms of behaviour and communication. Historians of Christian religion have a different task: liturgy (the principal repository of ritual forms) was a written code from an early stage, albeit one with substantial local variation. Their interest is in understanding the extent and power (or otherwise) of rituals such as the mass, public penance, blessings, and so forth. To what extent were the vast mass of lay people truly engaged by ritual conducted largely in Latin? How important to Christianity was ritual? Finally, in turning to civic ritual – often large-scale ritual involving a considerable number of participants – historians have been interested in analysing how towns and cities represented themselves to themselves and others; and whether rituals such as Corpus Christi processions worked to develop a sense of communal, corporate cohesion, or whether, on the contrary, they were occasions of hierarchy and tension.

There are many debates within and between these areas. One might argue that liturgy was not, in its regular, repetitive form, 'ritual' at all but only 'ceremony' – a distinction sometimes drawn by anthropologists between dynamic activities that negotiated change or renewal, and empty repetitions of a given script that simply announced the status quo. On the other hand, recent work on liturgy has emphasized precisely the power *of* repetition – of phrases and imagery that might well have gained greater familiarity through their continued use and re-use – and has emphasized the importance of the senses (hearing the liturgy sung, smelling incense, seeing candles lit, and so forth) in the overall experience.[8] There is argument also over the use of sources. Unlike anthropologists, medieval historians cannot talk with the objects of their study; we are limited to what a past writer (usually clerical) has chosen to record.[9] To return here to our opening example, the question is not so much whether the meeting between King Raoul and Duke William actually took place, as whether the apparent importance of the ritual elements reflects what all participants felt, or was something that the chronicler (Flodoard, in this case) wanted to emphasize. The ritual may loom larger than it should. Flodoard notes that negotiations took place, and these are surely also important. A rather similar interaction some 170 years later gives a fuller picture. Orderic Vitalis tells us of another two armies facing off, those of Henry I of England and his brother (and attempted usurper) Robert Curthose. Matters were again resolved with a fraternal embrace and a kiss, with no fighting; but it is clear that complex political negotiations dealing with matters well beyond personal status preceded this ritual conclusion, including the treatment of other dependent nobles, the transference of certain lands to Robert, the payment of a large annual fee, and a joint agreement to recover from other nobles certain lands formerly held by their father. It is certainly true that symbolic actions (another way of thinking about ritual) were part of it all: Orderic emphasizes that Robert and Henry stood alone and 'unattended' (i.e., as equals), in a large circle of their respective followers, and 'while all eyes were fixed upon them' concluded their discussion, embraced, kissed, and 'were reconciled'.[10] There was certainly an element of public performance here. But how does one balance the ritual element against the gritty negotiation of landholding and finance?

What, in any case, should historians do with ritual? One tradition has been to 'decode' specific rituals, often through recourse to other kinds of texts and imagery. Such an approach has been extremely helpful in shifting understanding away from the tendency to see medieval people as brutish, illiterate and crude. People waving swords around, throw-ing themselves to the floor, embracing each other, crying in public – all can be seen as means of symbolic communication, not signs of childish behaviour. In this sense, being sensitive and alert to ritual as meaningful action has greatly enriched our sense of medieval politics and culture. But 'decoding' can be problematic if taken too rigidly. What does a kiss mean? It can have several interpretations according to different kinds of ritual context, and may not, moreover, mean exactly the same thing to all observers of (or even participants in) a spe-cific ritual. Different contemporary observers can, indeed, 'read' rituals in quite different ways. Two chroniclers, Richer and Thietmar, record that after a defeat by Otto II in 978, the French moved the eagle atop the palace of Aix-la-Chapelle as some kind of ritual message to the Germans – only Richer thought that they turned it to the east as a gesture of menace to their neighbours, while Thietmar believed it turned west, peaceably directed to their own kingdom.[11] One might be tempted to see this as an effect of the problematic nature of early medieval chronicles and their sources of information, but consider a much later example: the Venetian ambassador to London and the Drapers' Company scribe both record in matching detail processions made by Londoners on the eves of the feast days of John the Baptist and St Peter and St Paul (24 and 29 June, respectively). The ambassador saw the ritual as a great collective communal rejoicing, uniting the city; the scribe depicts it specifically as 'the Mayor's Watch', a strongly hierarchical procession in honour of the civic oli-garch's officers, deployed in that year to keep strict order following certain tensions.[12]

Geoffrey Koziol has suggested that simply decoding a ritual in isolation is not terribly helpful: 'if we place it in a vacuum in order to observe it ... the experiment kills the ritual by isolating it from the complex set of related symbolic behav-iour' with which contemporaries would have been familiar.[13] More important, then, is to understand the wider system that any specific ritual fits into; and to see ritual behaviour as a 'language' of considerable breadth and depth, not simply a brief code-book. Anthropology has indeed encouraged histo-rians to think about ritual as something with almost infinitely extensible boundaries – gestures and other forms of symbolic communication not being limited to specific moments of ritual theatre, but suffusing life in general.[14]

The tale of the conception of King Jaime I of Aragon, told in the previous chapter, is hardly a 'ritual' that one can imagine being repeated; but it could be seen as containing ritual features, not only the obvious liturgical elements of prayer and masses, but also the submissive postures and weeping of those notables who burst into the king's bedchamber. Some historians have indeed argued that medieval emotions – at least those of princes and rulers, and as recorded by chroniclers – were more ritual and strategic displays projected outwards than uncontrollable reactions directed inwards.[15]

Another question, then, is, what did ritual do? Some of those studying medieval religion have, influenced particularly by the anthropology of Émile Durkheim, seen rituals as functioning to restore society to a balanced state. Acts of peacemaking, liturgical rites, fraternity feasts, civic processions, and so forth, work, it is argued, to activate feelings of community, either through collective representations of wholeness (Corpus Christi processions), projected symbols of sacrifice (the mass), or, in the case of unruly and carnivalesque celebrations, allowing the community to 'let off steam'.[16] 'Peacemaking', as a wider and often political activity, has been analysed through its ritual forms for a much broader area, stretching back to the realm of early medieval politics, into Scandinavian saga culture, to twelfth-century Italy and late medieval France, to mention but a few of the relevant studies.[17] However, work in these areas, and on civic ritual, has increasingly come to question the functionalist argument. Civic rituals were very frequently hierarchical, setting out the complex arrangements of rank within secular society; and, in the case of Corpus Christi processions and plays, there is clear evidence that violent argument about hierarchy could break out on precisely these occasions. Furthermore, a number of large-scale revolts were launched on or around grand annual ritual occasions, such as Corpus Christi or Midsummer: not only the events of 1381, discussed in Chapter 2, but also the French Jacquerie of 1358, for example. Occasions of collective ritual performance were a good time to launch insurrections, whether national or local, because the community was already geared up for collective mobilization, and the ritual context leant an additional weight of meaning (and, on occasion, possible excuse) to the political protest.

If ritual is a language, historians are increasingly seeing it as one through which arguments were conducted: a position proposed, countered, something altered in the process. Ritual can be seen not as a mystical recipe for transforming enmity, but as a set of possible (public) positions one can adopt, with a variety of potential outcomes. Moreover, ritual always frames the possibility of breaking the script and rewriting the action. Townspeople at Chambly in France went into the local woods, owned by the monastery of Pontoise, on Mayday 1311. But instead of simply gathering the small amount of greenery that custom permitted, they came in great numbers and stripped all that they could. Part of the motive may have been simple material need, but the ransacking was also a particular symbolic action – an assertion of collective strength by the commune – diverging from the existing customary script of subservience and charity.[18] Ritual can also be misunderstood, accidentally or deliberately. At the court of the east Frankish king Louis the German, at Frankfurt in 873, just after Christmas, Louis's son Charles jumped up and announced that he wanted to renounce the secular world, which, according to the chroniclers who recorded the event, occasioned much disruption and alarm. This may not quite be all it seemed, however: Charles, who had been plotting against his father, could have been attempting to enact a ritual of public penitence, in the hope of repairing tense political relations. Either his ritual went wrong, because it was enacted in the wrong way or at the wrong time, or the chroniclers deliberately misconstrued it, writing it up as an act of apparent madness in a calculated political move.[19]

Analysis of ritual is hence an ongoing part of medieval studies, and has been the site of some intense debate. Its centrality to certain areas of discussion, and its relatively recent entry into new ones (particularly analyses of late medieval high politics), ensure that it will remain so for some time to come. New currents in anthropology may spur fresh perspectives on existing examples, and a greater degree of comparison across the areas discussed here would undoubtedly prove productive. A medieval kiss is, at any rate, rarely just a kiss; communicative action and ritual performance suffuse our texts.[20]

Social Structures

'Feudalism' is a familiar word, but one that fragments upon closer inspection. Journalists and others sometimes use it pejoratively as a synonym for 'medieval' – some unfair working practices being 'positively feudal', for example. Adam Smith and Karl Marx labelled pre-modern societies 'feudal', based principally on what they saw as the essential economic structure of the period (arguably underestimating the extent of nascent capitalism associated with medieval cities). Even in modern historiographical deployment, its meaning is potentially multiple. Marc Bloch's *Feudal Society* used the term to define medieval society as one built upon vertical interdependencies, and more broadly to characterize the structure and *mentalité* of that society, arguing in fact for the existence of two different 'feudal ages', the first marked by the fall of Rome, the second by the eleventh-century growth of cities. Most influentially, 'feudalism' has been taken to denote either (1) the combination of landholding, patronage and affective personal relationships understood to constitute the hierarchical bonds between king, lords and knights; the lower party would perform an act of homage, making him the 'vassal' of his superior, while the latter might then bestow a grant of land (a 'fief') or office or other favour. The bond thus formed assumed a reciprocity of support, the superior supplying favours and protection, the inferior providing service (usually military) to his lord. Or else, following an essentially Marxist framework, (2) feudalism refers to the relationship between lord and subject peasant, the latter provided with land to work in exchange for labour service and subjection to financial exactions, and being in this sense 'unfree' (though not owned or without any rights, as a slave would be). Anyone born or marrying into an unfree family became subject to the same restrictions, and such 'serfs' were bound to the land, unable lawfully to choose to move elsewhere.

The latter situation has tended to be termed 'manorialism'

or 'lordship' in recent years, but its structure of vertical bondage and notional reciprocity invites continued thematic connection with the relationships between noble lords and vassals – this being precisely why Bloch wanted to describe a complete 'feudal' society. Another influential French historian, Georges Duby, argued also that the combination of lords, fiefs, vassals and homage was the product of a sharp change in medieval society around the turn of the eleventh century, brought about by the collapse of the Carolingian empire and other socioeconomic factors.[21] For Duby, these interpersonal agreements and affective relations took place in a period of governmental anarchy, and assumed the role that top-down, 'public' government had previously played. The wider implications of this last point – and some very important criticisms of it – will be explored later in this chapter, but here I want to focus on the issue of social structures and identities, for this is a theme that stretches beyond the specific discussion of 'feudalism' in current medieval history, taking in issues of civicness, family, gender, socioeconomic change and much else.

Duby's argument about a 'feudal revolution' in the early eleventh century was in one part based on the apparent rise in status of the warrior class who were the vassals – and hence muscle – of the lord. There had always been a social elite (an aristocracy) and there had always been warriors, but in certain times and places the warriors were more a class of specialized labour (as foot soldiers remained throughout the middle ages). However, knights – *milites* in Latin – were a new social group, and the twelfth and thirteenth centuries saw the further development of their identity and connections with lordship, into the formation of a noble class. Their status rose, and an accompanying ideology developed, based on Arthurian fantasy and ritualized martial practices such as the tournament. Thus knighthood not only raised the social level of mounted warriors, it also associated it with an ideology of social transcendence, where a knight and a lady were thought to be qualitatively different kinds of persons from an ordinary lay man or woman. This was in general the situation reached by the thirteenth century; in the late fourteenth and fifteenth centuries, a further transmutation occurred, as the very rich, mercantile elites in cities began to blur with their previously 'noble' superiors. These high bourgeois elites frequently adopted the chivalric symbols and ideology of knighthood, even if they had little or no involvement in actual martial practices.

Lower down the social scale, one can also discern social stratification, most obviously the complex differentiations between 'free' and 'unfree' peasants, but also the new social dynamics brought about by the development and growth of cities. In the twelfth and thirteenth centuries, medieval cities grew considerably: it is likely, for example, that Florence quadrupled its population during the thirteenth century, and at the end of that period it was forced to build new city walls some five miles in circumference. The movement of populations in and out of cities, the specialized industries that cities supported and, above all, the development of ideologies and associational forms connected with mercantile groups all meant that different social strata were produced. At the village level, in western Europe at least, the bureaucratization of royal power depended in part upon the establishment of local officials – bailiffs and reeves in England, *baillis* and *prévots* in France, for example – whose social status was thus raised.

The previous paragraph mentions not only different kinds of people, but ideas about different kinds of people. Historians have sometimes sought to establish an 'objective' social structure in a period – its bases in law, economics, power relations, and so forth – but always have to grapple with sources that more frequently present ideologies of social structure – the division of society into 'those who pray/those who fight/those who labour', the notion of chivalry, the disparagement of lower social classes as seen in the chronicle accounts of 1381. That there were social strata arrayed hierarchically is not doubted for any period; but how exactly they were arranged, and with what distinctions and implications, is a harder – and hence more intriguing – question. For the early middle ages, archaeological evidence provides clear grounds for discerning the division of society into elite and subordinate, on the basis of not only high-status treasure hoards and burials, for example, but also the differential arrangement of settlements and types of building. Documentary sources provide further clues – but, in the case of charters, the signs are frustratingly hard to decipher. One can track (as Duby did) the use of different specific terms to describe and differentiate social identities in such documents: *milites, caballarii, vassalli, fideles*, and so forth. But how one interprets these precisely may be dictated by the discursive context: 'vassal' in French vernacular literature of the high middle ages seems, for example, to mean something like 'courageous and loyal warrior' rather than anything specific to do with landholding and homage. Furthermore, the change in vocabulary may demonstrate a shift in scribal practices – the adoption of a new formulary – rather than any change in society itself.[22]

Legal sources may present glosses on social identities – definitions of unfreedom, for instance, or explanations of duties owed by a particular kind of person – and these can be extremely helpful. The twelfth-century law code, the *Usatges of Barcelona*, discussing penalties (a fine, and corporal punishment) levied for assaults, makes various distinctions and comparisons between levels of nobility. A viscount is worth two *comitores*, a *comitor* worth two *vasvassores*, and a *vasvassor* increases in value, as it were, for every knight beyond five that he holds. In another section, we are told that knights can have different ranks, possibly on the basis of whether they themselves have vassals. Most interestingly, the code states that a son of a knight is due the compensation of a knight up to the age of thirty; but if, by that point, he has not been made a knight, he is compensated only as a peasant. Moreover, anyone who 'abandons knighthood while able to serve it' is similarly judged as a peasant. Peasants themselves are noted only as those who hold 'no rank besides being Christian'; the latter in distinction to Jews and 'Saracens' (Muslims).[23] This gives us quite a full picture of social levels, and moreover the complexity of ideas about status, its assumed or achieved elements, the way in which it is worked out relationally, and its intersection with other cultural ideas about masculinity and religious identity. But one must also remember that it is an abstract set of ideas related specifically to a tariff of punishments. Whether, in a different context, Catalonian lords made the same fine distinctions between a *vasvassor* with five knights and one with ten knights is uncertain.

Moralizing ecclesiastical writers provide a different depiction of society, and from the later twelfth century this had particular pretensions towards including all social levels:

explanations of the particular sins to which different social groups were prone, for example, or *ad status* sermons directed towards specific audiences. These are again helpful, and can in some instances overlap and reinforce distinctions drawn in different sources, but once again are contextual. In the late twelfth century, Alain de Lille wrote *ad status* sermons directed towards soldiers, advocates, the married, widows and virgins.[24] These distinctions could certainly be made between lay people, but they clearly are not the only lens through which they were viewed. Taxation assessments – rare in earlier periods, but quite a rich source from the later fourteenth century – provide a more structured and economic basis for perceiving social strata. Detailed civic sources, for example in late medieval Ghent, allow historians to produce a picture of relative economic wealth among merchants, citizens and artisans, suggesting further refinements of socioeconomic structure. Making socioeconomic strata visible, literally visible through the clothing one wore, seems to have become a preoccupation of various late medieval cities and kingdoms, which passed sumptuary regulation often on the basis of income or birth. The modern historian Raymond van Uytven notes various ways in which one might chart medieval 'public opinion' on rank in the Netherlands, which might or might not correlate with economic position: the place given in processions or other public events, the quality of gifts given by urban governments to their visitors, the varied travel allowances permitted to official delegates, and sumptuary laws.[25]

From all of this, medievalists working across many different times and places have been particularly occupied with certain themes. The issue of nobility – rank as a matter not only of wealth but also birth – is one. The mechanisms, meanings and reactions against unfreedom are another. And issues of gender – particularly whether gender cuts across or supports social hierarchies – have provided a third. Let us take them in turn. The *Usatges* state that 'townsmen and burghers' are due the same compensation as knights, and that a bailiff (an officeholder) 'who is a noble, eats wheaten bread daily, and rides a horse' is compensated as a knight.[26] This gives an interesting mix of economic and ideological distinction: the ability to afford a horse and a certain diet, and the idea of being born noble. Nobility makes some difference (a bailiff of non-noble blood was due only half the compensation) but, on the basis of this particular tariff, raises an officeholder only to the same relative height as a city burgher. The idea of noble birth of course underpinned the pinnacle of medieval society, the king and his 'lineage'. That nobility and the potential for kingship were, in some times and places at least, understood to be transmitted through the blood gave a particular importance to noble women, with both positive and negative effects: women's status was in some senses high, but they were also pawns within a high-stakes marriage market.

However, while most of later medieval Europe had a nobility, to what degree their interests cohered as a class, and what the actual implications of nobility were, could vary considerably from place to place.[27] English Common Law made no substantial distinction between noble and non-noble; its main point of divide was between the free and the unfree. In the period after 1066, a key division was, understandably, between incoming Norman nobles and more or less subjugated indigenous people. In later centuries, the nobility as such were very clearly defined by admission to the House of Lords; but other 'gentry' families were also recognized as being above and different from the common folk. By way of contrast, for much of the middle ages Norway had no 'nobility' as such, but a very clearly defined group of *håndgangne menn* – 'men who have gone to the hands of the king' – to whom a different law applied than to others. However, in the fourteenth century, government officialdom separated from the king's immediate followers, and due to the unions made between Scandinavian countries, the king himself was frequently absent from the kingdom. In consequence, a much more 'European' ideology of nobility was imported – above all, the importance of bloodline rather than service – but to a much smaller and less influential group.[28] Nobility did mean privilege, but it did not always mean power. Noble families did not, in fact, necessarily survive very long: of sixteen families of the lesser nobility in twelfth-century Osnabrück, only six were still in existence by 1300; similarly, of seventy knightly families given fiefs in Eichstätt in the years 1125–50, only forty made it to 1220.[29] This suggests that 'nobility' had a wider ideological function than simply the sustenance of particular people's fortunes. It formed part of the medieval world's image of itself.

Not, however, that that image ever went unchallenged. As we have already seen, the English Rising of 1381 saw calls for universal manumission from serfdom, and criticism of lordship. This was far from the only occasion when such views were voiced: various rebellions across the middle ages demanded an end to unjust lordship (though not always necessarily its cessation), the common ownership of property and justice for all. What being 'unfree' meant was complicated, again varying by place and time. Historians have argued over different timescales for the enserfment of the common people. For Duby, it was part and parcel of the feudal 'revolution', occurring principally around the eleventh century (though as noted later in this chapter, this has become a hotly disputed topic). Others have suggested that it came about more steadily from the fall of the Roman Empire, with local landed warriors demanding service of those weaker people around them in return for 'protection'. By the thirteenth century, unfree peasants were bound to the land that they worked, subject to regular and arbitrary financial exactions, and required to render labour services to their lord. How harsh or otherwise these conditions were is also disputed; some have noted that bondage did supply some degree of protection in times of economic hardship, but others have argued that the lord's expropriation of the peasants' surplus labour rendered peasant existence perilous in the extreme. When a drastic drop in population levels occurred in the fourteenth century (through famine and then plague) it does seem to have signalled the beginning of the end of serfdom in some areas at least. But for some parts of Europe – notably Bohemia and Poland – the late middle ages saw a so-called age of 'second serfdom', with lords harshly reasserting dominance in the face of fourteenth-century change. The processes by which domination was achieved and sustained are key topics of study, and recent comparative work has brought to light the variations in experience across Europe (and, indeed, contrasts elsewhere in the pre-modern world, such as Japan). In Denmark, for instance, the peasantry had not been enserfed as in England,

France or Germany, and they mainly worked land held by leasehold for specific, relatively short, terms. It was, however, a tenet of Danish society that one needed a protector within law who was one's social superior. Changes in legal procedures in the thirteenth century paradoxically led to the peasantry becoming more dependent on, and tied to, landlords for legal protection. In northern Italy, in contrast, a similar period saw rural peasants moving from being tied to the land to a kind of 'share cropper' status known as *mezzadria*, while in Hungary the peasants remained obligated juridically to their lords in terms of services and dues, but from the thirteenth century were free in person, being able to move their labour elsewhere without restraint.[30] Historians have further discussed the roots of peasant resistance to these issues, arguing in part about patterns of socioeconomic fortune – for example whether, in the immediate aftermath of fourteenth-century plague, different groups were better or worse off – and also about whether peasants possessed something that Marxists would call a 'class consciousness', a sense, that is, of collective predicament and unity. Recent argument here has focused not only on large-scale popular revolt, but also on smaller-scale tensions at the level of the village.[31]

The paragraphs above, largely reflecting the past historiography and in part the sources, have tended to assume male knights, burghers and peasants. But what of women? They have sometimes been presented as, in the title of an influential book, a 'fourth estate' in medieval society, outside the normative tripartite structure.[32] But they were of course present at every level, and much work in the last few decades has been concerned with discussing what a recognition of their presence might do to our understanding of medieval social structure. The discussion differs, depending on whether one is looking at ordinary or noble women. In the lower strata of society – the vast majority of the medieval population – historians have investigated women's experience within the household and the workplace, thinking about their relative power and status, and the changes (if any) wrought by socioeconomic shifts over the centuries. Lifecycle has been noted as particularly important in women's lives: young women in northern Europe frequently went into service, which provided a degree of economic independence. Upon marriage, this shifted radically, as, although a collaborative model of marriage might pertain for many couples, the woman – in both law and the marketplace – was largely subordinated to the man. Widowhood brought further shifts: either a return and enhancement of independence if economically stable, or else a rather drastic fall into dependence upon others if not so fortunate. Comparisons between different parts of Europe are again apposite, the most important perhaps being a putative distinction between marriage models in northern and southern lands. In England and other parts of northern Europe, couples tended to marry fairly 'late' – in their mid-twenties perhaps, and with little or no age difference between them. In Italy and other southern areas, women tended to marry younger – maybe still in their teens – and to older men.[33] For elite women across Europe, something more like the latter model tended to hold sway. Analysis of this social stratum has looked at the power that women wielded within noble households, noting for example the common expectation that ladies would literally hold the fort in a husband's absence, and more broadly the implication of women as both agents and objects in power strategies of various kinds.[34] For all social levels, however, a key and continuing area of analysis is how status and gender combined. At one extreme, if we consider the extraordinary travels and encounters experienced by the outspoken late medieval mystic Margery Kempe, one may argue that her socially privileged background (daughter of a very powerful mayor of Bishop's Lynn) likely played a role in facilitating her adventures.[35] At the other, one can note that some elements of medieval misogyny, such as tales of violent and just retribution against sexually active women, were common across all social levels. *The Game of Chess*, a popular medieval text printed by Caxton, tells of how the emperor Octavian taught his sons to swim, joust and pursue other 'knightly' activities; while his daughters were to sew and spin 'and all other works belonging to women', in case they were ever impoverished. The section on 'The Queen' concludes with a tale of a regent who relinquished her besieged castle to the king of Hungary, on the promise that he would wed her. He slept with her for one night, then 'on the morn, he made her common to [i.e. raped by] all the Hungarians, and the third day after he did put a staff of wood from the nether

part of her through her body unto her throat or mouth'.³⁶
This she deserved, the text says, for her inconstancy and adultery. Even a queen could be subject to misogynistic horror; because, in the end, she was only a woman.

Globalisms

Towards the end of the later fourteenth century, as reckoned by the Christian calendar (the eighth century in the Islamic calendar), the Arab scholar Ibn Khaldûn wrote, among many other things, about what he saw as the fundamental conjunction of cities, trade and wealth in the expansion of governance. These things go together, he suggested, because cities make a great deal of labour available, which allows for the swifter accumulation of goods in surplus to immediate needs, thus facilitating trade, thus facilitating taxation, thus allowing rulers to expand their territories – including founding new cities, which allows the cycle to continue. He goes on to say:

> This may be exemplified by the eastern regions, such as Egypt, Syria, India, China and the whole northern region, beyond the Mediterranean . . . At this time, we can observe the conditions of the merchants of the Christian nations who come to the Muslims in the Maghrib. Their prosperity and affluence cannot be fully described here because it is so great. The same applies to the merchants from the East and what we hear about their conditions, and even more so to the Far Eastern merchants from the countries of the non-Arab Iraq, India and China. We hear remarkable stories reported by travellers about their wealth and prosperity.³⁷

Those first two sentences bridge regions that were at least 5,000 miles apart; the fourteenth-century world was more connected than one might assume. Granted, Ibn Khaldûn was an extraordinary thinker and a great traveller, whose personal experience in North Africa and the Middle East was more far-reaching than most. But in this one passage he mentions not only those peoples one might expect to find in contact via Mediterranean trade, but also people in the Far East; elsewhere in his great work, he displays knowledge of West Africa. As his own writings make clear – and as other evidence attests – the inhabitants of Europe and the peoples of the eastern edges of Asia were connected not only abstractly, within his panoramic theoretical reflections, but physically, by actual lines of trade; what we might call a 'world system' of interlocking networks, as Janet Abu-Lughod influentially described it some decades ago.[38]

Here, then, is a way of looking at the middle ages that is not geographically bounded by traditional kingdoms, still less modern nation-states, and which need not take the west European experience as its centre or starting point. A 'global middle ages', in potential at least. While fundamental academic scholarship on various aspects of the non-western pre-modern world has been pursued for over a century, often within 'area studies' departments, it is for the most part only in the twenty-first century that medieval historians have considered going 'global', picking up on a currently prevailing trend in wider, predominantly anglophone, historiography. But what we might mean by that, what implications it has for our methods, analytical tools and ultimate purposes, is still very much up for debate.

Ibn Khaldûn draws our attention to trade and the movement of goods and materials, and this is certainly a key area, of abiding interest and discussion. For centuries, silk cloth, and latterly raw silk, travelled from China to Italy (Lucca in particular), to be sold across western Europe. Linen travelled from western Europe to central Asia. Elephant tusks, mainly from central Africa, were traded to the Mediterranean and thence to both Europe and Asia. Pepper and ginger came from southern India and Sri Lanka to Venice, to be sold on at great expense; other precious spices came from even further afield to European markets, as did a variety of jewels such as diamonds and pearls.[39] All these and other items are testament to very long-distance travel and connection in the pre-modern world.

However, as reflection on the nature of the items just mentioned may suggest, transcontinental trade was mostly about very expensive products and materials, destined for very elite markets. One can draw lines out from this trade to a wider sociocultural field – for example, thinking of occasions on which non-elites may have been impressed by jewel-studded reliquaries or woven silk tapestries – but such lines will nec-

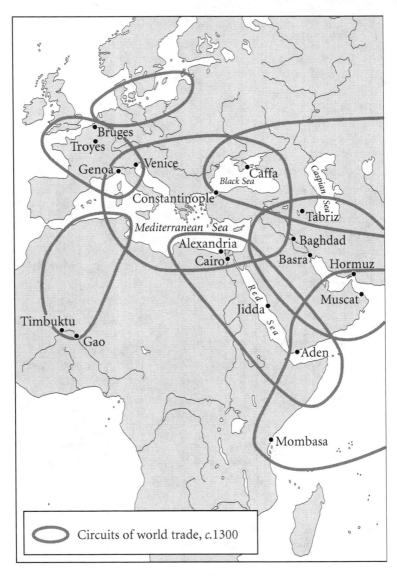

Map of 'World Systems, adapted from Janet Abu-Lughod's analysis

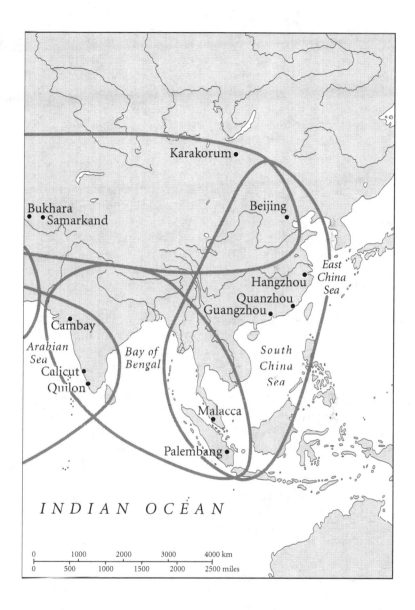

Karakorum•

Bukhara
• •Samarkand

Beijing
•

East
China
Sea

Hangzhou•
Quanzhou
Guangzhou•

•Cambay

Arabian
Sea
Calicut•
Quilon•

Bay of
Bengal

South
China
Sea

Malacca•

Palembang•

INDIAN OCEAN

0	1000	2000	3000	4000 km
0	500	1000	1500	2000	2500 miles

essarily be rather more like fine filaments than sturdy ropes. Moreover, the spice trade was really, as Peter Spufford put it, 'an Asian trade which was primarily in the hands of Asian merchants, with marginal European participation'.[40] One could make a parallel point about the 'Silk Road': although it did ultimately link western Europe to China, its more profound connections for most of the pre-modern period were between the Middle and Far East.[41] As Jan de Vries has argued with regard to early modern 'global' trade between Europe and Asia, long-distance exchange was relatively marginal to the main regional markets for these goods, and the nature of long-distance trade meant that commodities tended to change hands multiple times along the way, passing through a variety of 'nodal points' between different merchant communities, each adding to the opportunity costs of exchange. This, de Vries argues, meant that the wider 'globalizing' effects found in the modern period – the accompanying exchange of information, people, ideas, culture and, perhaps, convergence of economic systems – were mostly absent in pre-modernity.[42]

This is part of an ongoing unresolved debate among global historians of all periods, but it does suggest that medievalists should probably avoid slipping into any simple 'earlier than thou' position; what kinds of 'globalisms' we might explore for the pre-modern world are better served by being allowed their own specificity, rather than attempting simply to lay claim to the same overarching themes as our modernist colleagues. For example, we have long known that there are important intellectual exchanges, flowing from the Islamic to the Latinate world, in the eleventh and twelfth centuries, this being a primary route by which western Christendom came to engage with much classical learning. The environments within which these exchanges took place were part of the Mediterranean world, which in various locales – southern Spain, Sicily, Constantinople, the Crusader States – brought together (whether harmoniously or more conflictually) Arabs, Franks, Italians, Byzantines, Jews, and those from the various lands in northern Iberia and southern France. While trade was one highly important means of connection, court culture would appear to have been another; and studies of Mediterranean cultural exchange increasingly emphasize its political contours and limits, its tendency toward being a series of palimpsests more than an idealized 'melting pot'.[43] We might thus decide that the long-existing work on Mediterranean exchange is usefully viewed through a 'global' lens, with the potential to de-centre a European perspective and instead emphasize the connections between different peoples and regions. Drawing on Mediterranean experiences fulfils another aim of global history, in making particularly visible the presence of non-Christians within western Europe: the Jewish experience in Iberia (where recent work on the late medieval expulsion of Jews convincingly suggests that something very like modern 'racial' prejudice starts to operate around the subsequent 'purity of blood' discourse in Spanish culture) and elsewhere, but also the presence of North African people – particularly women – as domestic slaves in various cities around the Mediterranean, including in northern Italy and southern France.[44] This is not the same 'globalism' as one would find in the age of large-scale western colonialism, still less modern 'globalization'; but it is an important element to our understanding of medieval Europe, challenging problematic assumptions about its essential and unvarying 'whiteness'.

The archaeologist Ben Jervis has usefully suggested that, when looking at 'the global', the theoretical language of 'assemblage' – a somewhat transitory agglomeration of flows and connections formed by a particular nexus of power and desire – might provide a more useful explanatory metaphor for medievalists than the modernist language of 'structure' and 'network'.[45] In that fashion, we might see the extended medieval Mediterranean world presenting a sequence of different overlapping but largely separable 'assemblages', some for example. comprising sailors, wool and grain travelling by sea, connecting places as far afield as southern England, Algiers and Constantinople for a few centuries in the later middle ages; others built more from texts and travelling scholars, linking southern Spain, North Africa and the Crusader states over a somewhat earlier span of time.[46] We might then reflect on recent work that has emphasized connections in the medieval period between sub-Saharan West Africa – particularly the empires of Ghana, Mali and Songhay – and the Middle East, most famously in the pilgrimage route to Mecca taken by the great Malinese ruler Mansā Mūsā in the early eighth century (early fourteenth century by the Latin calendar), which included passage via Cairo, accompanied by 'vast wealth [borne by a] huge army' and many slaves, as a contemporary Arab source describes.[47] A line connecting West Africa to Mecca thus crosses over the lines connecting the Mamluk Sultanate to the Mediterranean and the Middle East, and thus a means by which Mansā Mūsā became known, for his fabulous wealth in gold in particular, to a much wider range of peoples including some in western Europe. These are connections, extremely interesting in themselves, and extremely important in understanding the history of West Africa in the pre-modern period; but they perhaps do not constitute 'an assemblage' of more than a very brief duration, still less a global 'network'.

Part of the point of global history more broadly has been to challenge grand narratives that unthinkingly place western Europe at their centre and as their default point of reference. Here, there are further medieval opportunities to explore. One might be to take the rise and spread of Islam as the main focus, to trace its flow westwards and eastwards (finding powerful converts in South-east Asia in the fourteenth century and after), seeing its particular conjunction of religious and political authority as the norm, rather than the confused and fragmented forms of kingship found in Europe, and considering whether – as Ibn Khaldûn would have seen it – the religion was the primary factor in 'civilizational' change, that is, in the settlement of cities, the development of trade, the elaboration of law.[48] In a different vein, R. I. Moore has suggested that all of Eurasia can be seen to undergo a period of great 'intensification', focused particularly on the tenth to the twelfth century, in terms of agricultural exploitation, civic settlement and economic activity, and accompanying political control by elites, creating a system of life sufficiently robust to survive the multiple global calamities of the fourteenth century.[49] In both cases, western Europe would have a place within the narrative, but would not sit by default at its centre. Both of those approaches, and doubtless others not considered here, would take us in the direction of a kind of 'grand globalism', which attempts to talk about historical forms and change in the most expansive fashion; though we would have to remind ourselves that it remains all but impossible to connect every area of the actual globe (to include the Americas and Australasia for example) to such a pre-modern vision.

But in any case, there are other possible approaches that one can take under the banner of 'global history'. One is to be comparative, for example via exploration of particular themes (gender, holiness, food cultures, kingship) or through examining the dynamics of similar technologies (writing, taxation, law). Here is a key extract from extensive writing carved onto a sandstone stela from tenth-century Khmer (modern-day Cambodia), found in 2013: 'In his [first] regnal year, this king of the Kambujas received tribute from the vanquished kings; but, being himself vanquished by devotion, he bestowed upon the [God] Śiva in this place the taxes which are to be levied annually from Lingapura'[50] In other words, the king (Īśānavarman II, d. 928 CE) was redirecting royal exactions to support this particular temple (at Vat Phu). The stela goes on to record the nature of the taxes owed to the king, paid in precious metals, animals, weapons, utensils, foodstuffs and other valuable items. Through want of other evidence, there are major challenges to understanding the wider dynamic within Khmer for this kind of activity. It has sometimes been seen as a sign of the Khmer state frittering away its own power, contributing to its eventual collapse. But, as Dominic Goodall argues, the support of monastic and hospital sites could also be seen as a means of strengthening infrastructure, a shared culture and local administrative influence. Exploring these possibilities can be aided by comparing such a royal action with what appear to be similar steps taken in other, western, kingdoms. This is what Goodall and Andrew Wareham do in the article from which I have drawn the Īśānavarman example, by looking also at exemptions from financial burdens granted by Mercian kings to various religious establishments in Kent. One could imagine a further comparison also with Carolingian habits of using monastic foundations as tools of empire. And there is an additional intriguing possibility presented by the precise language used – the elegant rhetorical reversal of the vanquishing king himself 'vanquished' by devotion – which would find close echo in other western examples, and might bear further analysis over the dynamics of the entwined legitimation of royal and spiritual power in the pre-modern world.

The 'global' is thus proving to be an important frame through which comparative medieval history – rather neglected until recently – can be reinvigorated. As various historians have noted, we must consider with some care which specific comparators are compatible, meaningful or useful to us, and there is also a slight worry that the allure of the new could lead to a loss of important contextual specificity; a danger of producing unwarrantedly 'thin' global comparators of the kind beloved by excitable popular economics books but rather less persuasive to historians. But good work is already being done, often through collaboration, sometimes through extensive engagement with anthropological as much as historical writings: for example, global comparisons regarding kingship and regnal masculinity, advice literature to rulers, religious asceticism and holiness, as well as more longstanding work on trade and economies.[51] The particular issue of the journal *Medieval Worlds* in which the Khmer/ Mercia article was published brought together highly illuminating work on the wider theme of 'religious exemption', an excellent topic for global comparisons, and in the process demonstrated that collaboration can work through publishing in proximity as well as through direct coproduction.

There are, however, some considerable challenges to pursuing medieval global history. One is whether we should be doing it at all under the 'medieval' heading: as discussed in the first chapter of this book, 'the middle ages' are part of a particular narrative periodization, one that emerges out of a western European experience and which is problematically tied to a particular valuation of 'development' and 'civilization'. While scholars of other parts of the world have sometimes adopted 'medieval' as a useable term, it should not be a label to which everyone unthinkingly defaults, as other periodizations, and possibly other terminology, may open up more productive perspectives (and may speak more resonantly to current political concerns).[52] Moreover, if we embrace the label 'global history' for the study of our pre-modern period, we must also decide to what extent, if any, we are attempting to engage in some of the key debates upon which modern global history has been centred: whether there was a 'great divergence' between the West and the East in the early modern period, whether forms of 'industrialization' characterize any pre-modern economies, and so forth. An important collection of essays on the 'global middle ages' explicitly attempts to reject a modernist frame of discussion, in favour of what it presents as thematic case studies, but the question of what our project really *is* still remains.[53]

Another challenge is the need for additional skills to traverse a wider range of cultures on an equal footing, the acquisition of a still wider range of languages being the most obvious. A sizeable portion of anglophone global modern history is pursued through a source base written in the dominant western languages of colonialism; the politics of this aside, for the middle ages that option mostly does not exist. More collaborative approaches between teams of researchers may therefore present a more practical route forward, though these bring their own challenges. A still further issue is the varied nature of the surviving source evidence. There are some parts of the world for which there are abundant and varied sources produced in the periods that interest us. China, for example, produced both official histories and a wealth of local written documents across many centuries, which can allow researchers not only to talk about the history of the elite ruling class, but to explore something of lived experience also.[54] In contrast, the only written sources surviving for Khmer across a similar period are sandstone stela, such as the one upon which Īśānavarman's monastic gift was carved. Archaeology provides another potential route of information, invaluable, for example, in understanding the extent of the Mayan civilization in South America prior to the Spanish conquest; but detailed archaeological investigation is, inevitably, patchy, as archaeologists cannot dig everywhere and cannot dig wherever they want. None of this makes global medieval history impossible, but it does mean that attempts to reach across a whole range of places, or to select synchronous global comparisons, have to negotiate very uneven evidential landscapes.

Naomi Standen, an historian of medieval Asia, has argued that '[w]hat makes a history global is precisely its refusal to sit within conventional bounds of nation-states, being prepared instead to follow the topic wherever it leads'.[55] Although admittedly, as noted in Chapter 1, the study of medieval history does bear the imprint of later nationalisms, it is fair to say that medievalists are in general rather more used to the idea that research need not assume the boundaries of 'the nation-state', and that meaningful areas of social, cultural and political analysis could both cross various regnal boundaries and equally exist in more micro-historical niches.[56] This parallels a point made by the great medievalist Eileen Power a century ago, following her own global travels: in not taking the modern nation-state as the pre-given frame, '[t]he Middle Ages are not mediaeval, in the sense of the politician, the journalist and the classical lecturer; they are ultra modern'.[57]

Cultural Identities

> [The civic leaders in Strasbourg] have set on high in the cathedral a certain boorish image under the organ, which they thus misuse: on the very sacred days of Whitsuntide . . . a certain buffoon hides behind that image and, with uncouth gestures and loud voice, belches forth profane and indecorous songs to drown the hymns of those that come in, grinning meanwhile and mocking at them . . . Moreover the Bürgermeister has his own place in the Cathedral, where he has been accustomed to talk with others, even when masses are being sung . . . Moreover, they commit other irreverencies also in holy places, buying and selling in the church porch . . . and bearing fowls or pigs or vessels through the church, even at times of the divine service.[58]

This account of impious and ribald behaviour in Strasbourg's cathedral comes from a letter to a papal nuncio written by Peter Schott, a clergyman in the city, in about 1485. The compositional context is complicated, bound up with a particular dispute between certain religious reformers and the ecclesiastical and secular authorities in the city. Schott's picture of lay abuses was thus part of a propaganda battle. It also conflates a specific, annual practice linked to the Whitsun festival – the mocking image – with what is likely a more regular, and highly common, lay appropriation of sacred space for mercantile and social activities.[59] But the image it conjures of a rumbustious, impious, profane laity clashing with the solemn and sacred power of the Church has a much wider resonance.

The Russian theorist Mikhail Bakhtin, writing in the early twentieth century, saw episodes such as this as a sign of cultural divergence, an important gap between a monovocal, official, sacred culture and a heteroglossic, popular, 'low' culture of the masses.[60] Looking to other medieval episodes, such as the persistence of folk magic, the veneration of springs and other unofficial shrines, the belief in non-Christian supernatural entities, or occasions when orthodox faith was apparently mocked or subverted, various historians have taken the theme of cultural division as a key interpretation in the study of medieval religion. Jean Delumeau famously argued that the middle ages were 'barely christianized', the elements of apparent orthodox devotion forming a mere veneer over an essentially pagan underbelly.[61] Similar, albeit less extreme, views have been propounded by other French medievalists, notably Jacques Le Goff and his student Jean-Claude Schmitt: that there were important differences between 'official' and 'folk' (rather than 'pagan') cultures, although the two were not utterly separable, and intertwined in important ways. Nor were these cultural differences only religious: Le Goff has argued for a shift between 'church time' and 'merchant time' in the late medieval period, for example.[62]

Anglophone historiography has tended to push in the opposite direction, for some time explicitly wedded to the image of a medieval 'Age of Faith' and devout credulity, but more recently and subtly insistent on the specifically medieval nature of pre-Reformation Christianity, arguing for its own vitality and depth. Some historians have suggested that there was little or no difference between 'folk' and 'official', or 'popular' and 'elite', religion.[63] The extent to which the clergy were, particularly at the parochial level, deeply connected with the secular community has been increasingly emphasized; late medieval sermons on marriage from Poland, for example, indicate considerable understanding of, and sympathy for, the realities of everyday lay life.[64] Opinion is thus divided. Two aspects to this argument within religious history link the area to wider medievalist debates: the nature and importance of cultural divisions, and the means and effectiveness of acculturation (the successful dissemination and sustenance of a particular, dominant world-view).

We saw earlier some ways in which medieval society was

divided by social hierarchy, and how these strata arguably changed over time. The kind of 'division' explored here is not unconnected to those issues, but is at a more profound level: whether various parts of medieval society had fundamentally different world-views, cultural mores or *mentalités*. A particular division emphasized by narrative sources from quite an early period is that between *litterati* and *illitterati* – literate and illiterate. As we have seen, to be a *litteratus* implied knowledge, learning and wisdom, and was largely synonymous with *clericus*. The *illiterati*, on the other hand, were also the *rustici*, the *simplices*, the *idiotae*.[65] Without sharing the disparaging sense implied by these terms, various modern historians have seen this perceived division as an essential fault-line running through the middle ages. Following the work of some influential anthropologists (as discussed in Chapter 3), certain historians have argued for elements of fundamental difference between oral and literate cultures, the former recursive and fluid, the latter capable of cumulative knowledge and reflection, and the development of bureaucratic mechanisms of power.[66] Our access to 'oral' or 'popular' culture can come, however, almost only through written sources, and historians have emphasized how intertwined, within those materials, the spoken and the written become; and moreover, the clear importance that 'oral' cultural elements – such as custom – had within 'official' culture.[67]

There is also the issue of change over time. To return specifically to the religious question, we know for a fact that, in the early centuries of Christian conversion, pre-Christian religious practices, rituals and places persisted within the general populace. This was in large part because 'conversion' initially meant a change of policy by the relevant local ruler, and mechanisms for instructing and acculturating the general populace into the new faith were initially sparse. A principal tactic by early Christian proselytizers was to transform existing pagan sites or temples into Christian ones. It is probable that this did, in fact, fairly swiftly erase pre-Christian theological ideas and religious rituals.[68] But it arguably preserved a deeper continuity of practice and expectation, the use of certain shrines for healing, for example, or the performance of particular rituals of protection relating more to a sense of 'good fortune' than to Christian eschatology. By the thirteenth century, it is clear that the Church was expending considerable energy on instructing the laity through preaching and a well-endowed parochial system of spiritual care. Thus, by the time Peter Schott was writing his letter about practices in Strasbourg, any sense of 'pagan' survival is surely unhelpful. The lay practices he decries are more like grotesque manuscript marginalia, used to define the ordered central space of the Christian text.[69] More interesting is the issue of how local cultures became Christianized – and the degree of variation that persisted within this notional uniformity. The use of ritual practices, visual imagery, preaching and other pedagogic techniques all played a role. The means by which cultures are produced and reproduced has been pursued in other areas also, such as the development of post-Roman 'barbarian' identities, and the imposition of a 'Carolingian' culture.[70]

Recent writers have tended to argue that what marked medieval Christianity most particularly was its relatively universal character and shared practices, expressed within local variation. Even those elements one might initially see as 'folkloric' – such as blessing fields or ploughs to ensure a good harvest – can be seen as deeply Christian in that they deployed Christian prayers, often employed the services of a priest, and were performed at times in the ritual calendar that was, whatever its originary rhythms, by the thirteenth century clearly 'Christian' time. Most Christians of whatever status went to mass; most said prayers; most attended confession; most were baptized, and received Extreme Unction on their deathbed. The point can be expanded to encompass other aspects of culture: ritual customs such as 'Maying' were practised up and down the social scale, from the village to the royal court. Late medieval vernacular literature was not restricted to the nobility, and reached at least some way down the social scale. Collective activities such as civic processions or legal courts or religious confraternities involved people across many social strata. The cultural idea of 'chivalry', notionally particular to one social class, can be seen in the fourteenth and fifteenth centuries (and indeed beyond) to be something attractive to non-nobles, particularly mercantile elites who adopted or appropriated elements of its symbology in their self-representation.[71] It has been argued that the social theorizing of Parisian theologians – surely the pinnacle of the *litterati* – was deeply informed by their contact, through preaching and the administration of confession, with ordinary lay people.[72] Even medieval heretics and their supporters shared large elements of religious imagery and practice, as much as they diverged from the culture of their orthodox neighbours.[73]

However, one might read some of these examples of shared culture in a slightly different way: as evidence for how successful, over time, dominant culture was at acculturating other social groups. If Christianity became a shared culture, it did so through the Church's efforts, embodied particularly in the activities of the mendicant orders, some reformist bishops and a reinvigorated system of parochial care. One must remember, moreover, that even at the end of the middle ages, the bulk of the surviving evidence tells us principally about the higher ranks of society. Recent work on literacy has emphasized the existence of a much higher level than some older historiography had assumed, starting with the Carolingian empire, and noting later particular peaks of vernacular literacy in northern Italy, southern France, Scandinavia and large cities throughout Europe. This has, in turn, helped to question hard and fast assumptions of cultural division, and encouraged the use of literary sources as evidence for shared cultural mores across social classes. But one must be wary: much more literacy than previously assumed is not the same thing as general literacy. In a similar fashion, evidence for greater overlap between religious practices than previously assumed is not the same as complete overlap. In both cases, something may be lost in the move from one paradigm to another. While books of hours, for example, were certainly a very common feature of late medieval lay religiosity, they were a feature still restricted by and large to a limited, mostly civic, elite. As we saw in discussion of the 1381 rising, medieval chroniclers could see themselves as members of a political and literate elite, and their negative views on the 'rabble' below them could lead to cultural misunderstanding. The evidence of certain inquisitorial trials indicates both the presence of some very unorthodox and arguably 'folkloric' beliefs and, perhaps more interestingly, the vibrancy among non- or semi-literate groups of storytelling and gossip, the latter being an element of 'oral' culture that only enters the historical record at extraordinary moments.[74]

We must therefore be alert to the possibility of cultural difference, and think carefully about the contexts (social, evidential, chronological) within which cultural mores were expressed. Recent work on attitudes towards sex and sexuality in the period have interestingly drawn out strands of similarity and difference, noting the influence of ecclesiastical viewpoints on social concerns with sexual immorality, but also indicating ways in which lay ideas could vary, showing greater tolerance for unmarried sexual activity at times of economic prosperity, for example, or, in some parts of Italy, largely excluding clerical involvement in marriage ceremonies.[75] Study of medieval preaching and religious art highlights the importance of what literary scholars would call 'reader response theory', the necessity of thinking not only about the message intended by the author or preacher, but the ways in which such a message was likely to be received, and the importance of mapping the potentially different ways in which it could be understood. While the theological culmination of the mass was the elevation of the Host, it has been argued, for instance, that for some lay people the moment of making offerings or saying personal prayers could, for them, have been the focus of the ritual.[76] More anthropologically inspired research has emphasized the number of potentially competing conceptions of 'sainthood' at play in canonization proceedings, and the varying cultural contexts and interests they indicate.[77] Such contexts and cultures were clearly not hermetically separate from each other – indeed, as Laura Smoller has demonstrated, the expectations of the (literate, clerical) investigators could, over time, shape the ways in which canonization witnesses 'remembered' their testimony for the written record – but they remain different spheres of cultural association.[78] Moreover, for some historians, the process of communication or education between clergy and laity should be seen as an operation of power, the imposition over time of an ecclesiastical hegemony in terms of morality and social order.[79] With this thought, we turn to our final section.

Power

In the summer of 1306, on the order of King Philip IV, all the Jews in France were arrested. Their property was confiscated, their families rounded up, and they were expelled from the kingdom; a group perhaps some 150,000-strong. Many headed south, to the Iberian Peninsula, or east, to Italy. This was, sadly, far from the nadir of Jewish/Christian relations in the middle ages. There was no accompanying popular violence or pogroms, no programme of anti-Semitic preaching, as there had been before and would be again. Philip IV's actions do not particularly stand out amid the broader history of hatred. But they arguably do present a remarkable moment in the exercise of royal power, deployed through an extensive and well-organized machinery of governance. Philip's officials were commanded directly by the throne; the plans for the expulsion were drawn up some weeks in advance of the deed, but successfully kept secret; and the seizure of people and goods was achieved with notable uniformity and great swiftness.[80]

But just a few years earlier, another event from Philip's reign gives a very different picture of governance and authority. In 1300, the king had imposed a tax to fund his ongoing campaign in Flanders. As happened throughout the kingdom, a royal official consequently toured the administrative area surrounding Carcassonne to collect the tax. At the town of Foix, in the Pyrenean foothills, he found himself physically barred from entry and the inhabitants unresponsive to threats of royal authority. Moving on to the town of Varilhes, he managed to extract some money and set off back to Carcassonne. En route, however, he was waylaid by the *bayle* (local official) of Foix and some others, who took the money and his belongings, and sent him on his way. Once back at the city, the royal official sent two sergeants to summon the inhabitants of Foix for contempt; but they too were barred from entry, and were then beaten up at another village. In subsequent years, the counts of Foix refused royal orders to hand over the perpetrators, or indeed to accede to the tax. Eventually, the French crown gave up trying.[81]

The theme of this section is not the degree of power wielded by Philip IV of France. Rather, the two examples from his reign highlight two poles of possibility across the whole medieval period that play key roles in larger debates, and have implications for the study of power not only at a royal level. The example of the Jewish expulsion underlines the power of bureaucracy, centralized control and the potential for the arbitrary intercession of the state throughout the realm. That of Foix demonstrates lack of effective authority at every social level, the limited resources of force at royal disposal and the difficulty of actually collecting taxation. One could multiply the examples from other times and places: the successful expansion of the Carolingian empire, set against its limited ability to control the peripheries of its realm; the centralization of royal justice in Henry III of England's reign, versus his problems in controlling baronial rebellion in the 1250s and 1260s. For a long time, medievalists tended to think about this spectrum of power in terms of the 'strength' or 'weakness' of individual kings – tending, like the chronicle sources that informed their studies, to associate this to some degree with quasi-moral qualities inherent in the particular monarch – and more broadly to place these judgements within a particular narrative of the rise of the state. Once upon a time, it was said, there was the Roman Empire, a strong and efficient state, with a centralized bureaucracy, taxation, standing armies and a consequent monopoly on order. When it collapsed, Europe was plunged into governmental darkness, where the only authority came from the sword of whichever local warlord fought his way to the top of the heap. Then the Carolingians came along, and provided a new 'empire' that had at least a modicum of centralized governance. But this too fell (or was frittered away), and around the turn of the eleventh century a period of feudal anarchy ensued, with localized warlords again holding sway. Finally, across the twelfth to the fourteenth century, strong monarchs, particularly in France and England, developed centralized, bureaucratic states that provided a stable system of governance and law. These in turn fostered parliamentary powers and led to constitutional monarchies. The foundation stones for the modern state had been laid.[82]

In recent years, however, this tale has come under multiple attack. Various faults are noted: the tendency for French and English experiences to be taken as the dominant paradigm for all Europe, the teleological nature of the narrative, the assumption that centralized, top-down authority is obviously 'better' than decentralized and localized power (or indeed that top-down authority has the 'best interests' of those it governs at heart). Dominique Barthélemy and others have challenged Duby's claim for a swift period of eleventh-century 'feudal revolution', a perspective largely embraced by British medievalists; while other French and American scholars have pushed back, and continue to argue for some form of fundamental transformation across the high middle ages.[83] Most productively, historiography has moved away from debates about the merits or demerits of particular individual rulers, and has started to think instead about the nature and effectiveness of different elements of rule, and how these changed over time. 'Kingship' is increasingly seen by new strands of political history not as a quality inherent in specific individuals, but as a construct of political culture and a structural component within wider mechanisms of dominion. Moreover, what we mean when we talk about a 'state' in the medieval period has been much discussed. All are agreed that it was at no point identical to the modern 'nation-state' – although there is much argument as to whether or not some idea of 'nation' did pertain in various European countries (again, notably, England and France). Different requisites for potential statehood have been noted: the tools to raise regular finance, the maintenance of social order, the ability to intervene at will regardless of geographical and customary variations, the degree to which governance operates independently of direct personal engagement by the ruler. A further question is the necessary degree of interrelation between these elements – how does one square a relatively strong system of royal justice and a relatively weak system of centralized taxation, as in thirteenth-century France?

Certain historians have suggested that tax – or, more broadly, the ability to raise regular revenue – must lie at the heart of any discussion of medieval statehood. For the early middle ages, a key debate has been over degrees of continuity in governance after the apparent 'fall' of the Roman Empire. In a synthesis of the historiography, Chris Wickham has argued that some areas – most notably North Africa and

Byzantium – retained elements of the Roman apparatus of taxation, whereas others – Britain being a key example – did not. The ability to tax depended upon information gathering and record keeping, means of cooperation between localized and centralized officials, and an acceptance of regularized coercion. In those lands where the Roman system was abandoned, it took tremendous effort to build anything comparable afresh – such an effort, in fact, that one did not see it in much of Europe for many centuries. A strong taxation system did not guarantee a 'strong' state with regard to all matters – Byzantium in the early middle ages was not able to bat away external pressures – but it made possible modes of governance to which other kingdoms could not aspire.[84] In a study of later periods, Mark Ormrod has suggested, with regard to finance, that we could helpfully think about different kinds of 'state', arguing for a fourfold typology of 'tribute' state, 'domain' state, 'tax' state and 'fiscal' state.

Thus, while the Anglo-Saxon and Norman states did use forms of taxation, these were always applied extraordinarily, and basic royal revenue derived instead from demesne lands and regalian rights. For Ormrod, this makes them 'domain' states. In England, the key change comes only in the mid-fourteenth century, with the introduction of permanent forms of indirect taxation (on overseas trade) and a more frequently imposed direct taxation (on moveable property); at this point, the realm moves to being a 'tax state'.[85] The ability to impose tax, of whatever kind, has itself a complex relationship with other kinds of regnal power. It was common in later medieval Europe for a ruler to grant exemptions from certain taxes to particular corporate groups, most often cities, in exchange (explicitly or implicitly) for other forms of political support. While the consequent growth in civic independence could be seen, in the short term, as a diminution of centralized power, it has also been argued that the governmental machineries developed in precisely these urban settings played a key role in later state development. Equally, in some situations rulers could grant an element of financial autonomy to local areas to promote economic activity and trade, while retaining taxation rights over the subsequent trading routes – as was the case under the Sforza and Visconti nobles in fifteenth-century Tuscany.[86]

Beyond all this however is a still wider question. As Patrick Wormald has put it, 'Power is the staple of modern historical discourse ... Yet, when asked what they mean by power, historians can look shifty.'[87] To answer this, one must look beyond the specific machinery – a taxation system, a jurisdictional area, and so forth – to the ways in which such elements were permitted to operate in the first place. And the question can in fact be widened from the issue of royal or governmental power, to encompass the broader realms of medieval society – the power wielded by nobles over commoners, the power wielded by civic elites over city-dwellers, the power wielded by the Church over Christendom, and power at its most local levels, in the villages and parishes and households.

First, violence. It would be wrong to depict medieval society as characterized by constant violence. But it is clear that the possibility of violence – and its intermittent strategic enactment – played a role in the creation and maintenance of political systems at all levels. Whether we are in a world of small-scale minor lordships, or broad, cross-boundary 'empires', the ability to inflict decisive physical force was a common factor in control. Frankish expansion in the eighth century began, at the very least, through military victory, and resistance to the empire, such as the sworn conspiracy of central German landowners in 786 against Charlemagne, could be met with violence both real and symbolic: the ringleaders were blinded and executed. There are several reasons why Lithuania was brought within late medieval Christendom or Wales under English royal control, but pre-eminent was the use of military force. The potential for, and periodic reality of, horrific violence characterized relations between lords and peasants also. Orderic Vitalis tells us that, in 1124, Count Galceran of Meulan punished peasants who had illegally cut wood from his forests by having their feet amputated. Felix Hemmerli, a mid-fifteenth-century writer in Zurich, recommended that peasant farms be razed to the ground once every fifty years or so, in order to prevent them from becoming 'arrogant'.[88] Such actions were not constant, and as a strategy could backfire – one might argue that it was precisely the harshness of serfdom in fifteenth-century Germany that sparked major peasant rebellions and the sixteenth-century 'Peasants' War' – but the threat of violence was ever present.

Violence could come from central authority, such as royal justice, from within local hierarchies, such as the lord and his men, and from communal sources, as when people were subjected to humiliating public penances for fornication or adultery. Individuals attempting to maintain 'honour' had recourse to violence – in 1479, one Fritz Schreppler attempted to cut off his wife's nose in the marketplace in Nuremberg, both a physical assault and an act of symbolic meaning, as various similar cases attest.[89] Part of what kept the medieval social order in place at all levels was physical force, and the meanings given to violent action.[90]

Another set of tools, connected in some ways with the above, was the bestowal of patronage and the cultivation of personal charisma. Much work has been done on the former topic, in older work on institutional structures and kingship, and in recent historiographies that take a more anthropological view of power. The process of patronage – bestowing office, lands or favours in return for political support – is familiar across medieval politics, from the creation of the Carolingian empire, to the activities of various Emperors in the German lands, to the consolidation of the Capetian kingdom under Blanche of Castile. Studies of civic oligarchical elites indicate similar systems of patronage and kinship networks at a more local level, and one suspects that further work lower down the social scale would provide yet more. Understanding how patronage operated in part leads us back to issues of social structuration, but also directs us towards interactions of secular with ecclesiastical spheres of power. In the eighth to the eleventh century, in particular, it has been argued that the large degree of secular patronage of the Church (particularly in the form of monastic endowments) demonstrated not only piety on the part of lords, but also political manoeuvrings. In part, the point of patronage was to demonstrate, not only to the donee but to others too, that one was capable of bestowing it. (This was similarly the case with later medieval guilds: by banding together, more lowly people became capable of acting collectively as patrons, gaining some of the social cachet this implied.)[91] As recipients of patronage, monasteries themselves became political players of major importance – Cluny perhaps being the most famous, but others also, such as Bury St Edmunds, Redon and St Bertin. As discussed in Chapter 2, medievalists have been reflecting in these areas on the complex nexus of obligation, expectation and assumed kinship in the concept of 'the gift'. What nobles received back from monasteries was not simply spiritual sustenance, religious kudos or practical assistance (although all those things surely were in play); they were also binding themselves in ideological ways to the sense of charismatic power embedded in monastic shrines, with a hope that such *fidelitas* might assist their own operations.[92] Religion in a broader sense – the standing implied by adherence to good Christian practices such as charity – pervaded late medieval civic politics also: by the fifteenth century, most oligarchies in each north European city were members of the same guild. Personal charisma, that rather indefinable sense of individual magnetism that has long exercised sociologists and political advisers, was clearly possessed by some secular leaders – William Marshall springs to mind, and Henry V of England – but it perhaps most frequently worked through religious resonances, such as modelling one's behaviour on the apostles, or other pious exemplars. The succession of charismatic preachers who shook the politics of late medieval Italy – John of Vicenza, Bernardino da Siena, Savonarola – were undoubtedly remarkable men, but also men shaped by a notably similar mould. Making use of such charismatic qualities was another tactic available to medieval rulers, most famously perhaps in the Dauphin Charles's use (and then abandonment) of Joan of Arc.

Linked with charisma, but more programmatic, was the use of symbolic practices and the development of particular ideologies of power – both, again, primarily using religious ideas and imagery. The most famous case here is that of the Capetian monarchs who, Marc Bloch argued, imbued their kingship with sacral elements such as being anointed 'king', investing heavily in holy relics, and claiming a quasi-sacramental power principally through the 'Royal touch'. One might see a parallel tactic in the late medieval use of Arthurian chivalric imagery – another charismatic model – in the pursuit of royal aims, most famously in Edward III's creation of the 'Order of the Garter' in 1348; and it has indeed been argued that the Capetian and Plantagenet monarchs thus developed two contrasting models of kingship, the former 'sacral', the latter 'chivalric'.[93] How 'sacred' imagery became associated with kingship – and whether the two terms are easily compared across the early and later middle ages – has been further debated.[94] Various rituals, as discussed above, clearly performed and reproduced social hierarchies and power. Explicit ideologies of power and hierarchy were also found throughout the middle ages, from texts loosely known as 'mirrors for princes' which proffered advice to rulers, to more abstract treatises on the nature of politics, influenced by Aristotle's *Politics* (a text made available to a western audience through Latin translation in the later thirteenth century). John of Salisbury's image of the medieval polity as a body is perhaps the most famous, and one of the most pervasive, ideological statements of power and reciprocity. Its resonance and persuasive force rested in large part on placing a natural image at the heart of a political ideology, one that could be reproduced visually and that had potential emotional affect at all levels of society. Other strands of ideology similarly worked by associating a right ordering of the universe with God, nature and the experience of history. Gender played a key role here, particularly in the other common image for the polity as a household: just as man ruled woman, so the king ruled people, and so on. Political tensions could be signified in gendered terms, at many levels of society. A thirteenth-century public mural of a tree festooned with disembodied penises, in the Tuscan town of Massa Marittima, associates the incursion of Imperial power with images of sodomy, communal violence and the magical emasculation of men by witches.[95] Another image of potential power – the idea of the 'nation' – has been discussed in relation to the medieval period, with particular attention paid to the English case. John Gillingham and Patrick Wormald have argued for a long-held sense of 'Englishness' that could be used as a political resource in certain disputes.[96] This sense of 'nationhood' was not identical to modern nationality (and the kingdom not identical to the nation-state) but the degree of alleged difference has been disputed.

The biggest challenge for medievalists, with regard to 'the nation' and 'the state', is to think about these topics within their medieval setting, rather than as pale foreshadowings of later developments – or, indeed, seeing those later developments (pre-eminently the modern nation-state) as the only necessary, conceivable and meaningful outcome of the medieval period. Matthew Innes has argued strongly that power in early medieval politics was innately interpersonal, and that conceptions of 'statehood' that emphasize only the abstract or impersonal elements of rule fundamentally misunderstand its nature.[97] The development of textual, bureaucratic machineries of government (associated particularly with northern Italy, France and England) has been much studied, and historians have argued for their roots in monastic practices of recordkeeping, the extension of papal models of government, the propagation of royal chancery techniques, and so forth. But others have also argued against assuming a 'top-down' imposition of 'the state' (for good or ill) and its machineries, suggesting that much of what looks familiar to modern governmentality comes more from the bottom up, from local practices of notarial culture, parochial or village government and conflict resolution.[98] A parallel can be seen here with the other side of the issue, in studies of popular resistance to power, such as the 1381 rising or smaller and more localized revolts. An older historiography tended to read such events in the light of future forms of popular political resistance, and hence rather despaired of the apparent failure of medieval peasants to forge a collective politics of class identity or coherent programme of political reform. But recent work has looked much more sympathetically on the ways in which specifically medieval ideas of collective justice – some based on religious models, though some not – informed resistance; and has seen more low-level resistance than previous generations recognized, and also the involvement of non-elite groups in issues thought of primarily in terms of royal politics.[99] Power – and opposition to power – has at all levels become a far more complex topic for medievalists in the last few decades.

5
Making and Remaking the Middle Ages

When I see men of the present time, hard-pressed by misfortunes, anxiously scanning the deeds of their predecessors for consultation and strength, and unable to get as much as they wish, I conceive it will be a great service to posterity to commit to writing the deeds of the present for the use of the future.

Eadmer, *Historia novorum*[1]

Around the time I began writing the first edition of this book, we had some wood delivered at home in order to make bookshelves. As I helped the delivery man unload the timber, he asked me what I did for a living. 'Medieval history', I said. 'Oh', he replied. 'Right . . . Much call for that, is there?'

Despite his doubtful tone, the question rather pleased me. It implied the possibility of an artisanal approach to studying the middle ages – a jobbing medieval historian called in to fix a particular kind of problem, implicitly standing alongside other skilled trades. This might not reflect the experience of real academic careers, but it had a certain allure, partly because of its resonance with the English title of Marc Bloch's great work of historiographical instruction, *The Historian's Craft*. If, however, we are not able to justify our practice in the same terms as a cabinetmaker or silversmith – or indeed as a trade self-evidently important to modern society, such as refuse collector, surgeon or advertising executive – how does one account for what we do? Is there much call for medieval history, and, if so, in what terms, and to what ends? In this final chapter I want to reflect briefly on the uses of medieval history, the different purposes to which we can make and remake the middle ages, and the continued importance of so doing, not only to other historiographies but also to society more broadly.

For Eadmer (*c*.1060–*c*.1128), the answer was easy. One writes history for posterity – by which he meant, along with many others before and after him, for future rulers. The idea that history provides a 'storehouse of examples', particularly for statecraft, is perhaps its oldest justification. In modified form, it has continued to be invoked in recent times. For instance, in 1988 the great medievalist Richard Southern argued that the past that he studied provided us with a 'treasure of unused wealth', particularly from a spiritual perspective.[2] But such an argument has always been problematic for medievalists, because the very formation of 'the middle ages' – the cutting away of the period between the Fall of Rome and the Renaissance – depended upon an act of disavowal. Those early-modern writers and thinkers who encouraged us to think of that millennium as 'medieval' did so by asserting its discontinuity from, and essential irrelevance to, coming modernity. How can one persuade 'posterity' (whomsoever we now consider to populate that category) that it can make future use of examples drawn from a time instrinsically understood to be irrelevant? Only, it might seem, if the examples are all brutally negative ones; that is, by continuing to assert the difference and inferiority of the period, in a viciously circular argument. Such attitudes continue to inform, in subtle fashion, much of the contemporary world's view, both popular and intellectual: plenty of books addressing 'essential' human characteristics begin with the Greeks and the Romans, and then jump swiftly to the Renaissance or Enlightenment, confident that anything in the middle has little relevance. It also underlies the periodic assertion that we are living in a 'new middle ages', usually diagnosed by a breakdown in centralized authority and degraded forms of culture. Such Cassandra-like prophecies operate through exactly the same process of disavowal: they warn us against being like the middle ages, because such a fate would all too clearly signal the collapse of all we hold dear. There is also an occasional manifestation of the

apparent reverse of this view, a highly conservative yearn-
ing for a new middle ages of deference and accepted social
hierarchy. The politics of this aside, it falls prey just as much
as negative views to a homogenized and distorted notion of
the period.[3]

There is, however, another strand of medievalism, in
European culture in particular, which looks to the period
as an important source of origins. Nationalist elements of
this were mentioned in Chapter 1, but there is more here
than simply the earlier triumphalist narratives of individual nation-states. Various social and political entities that
continue to structure the world today can be traced back
to the middle ages. The most well-established area is perhaps political constitutionalism, which, in the nineteenth
and early twentieth centuries, was particularly fond of tracing an unbroken line between modern political mechanisms
and medieval precursors, the English Parliament being the
pre-eminent example. Recent work on medieval politics has
much more nuanced things to say here, about the nature of
'parliament' in medieval England, the similarities and differences between those parliaments and the contemporary
French *parlements* and Iberian *cortes* (Aragon in fact gained
an annual parliament earlier than other west European countries), the degree to which medieval politics recognized anything like an abstract constitution, the complex competitions
of power involved in the periodic limitations placed upon
monarchy, the web of interpersonal relationships and local
networks of patronage that affected the implementation of
national policies, and so on and so forth. These matters do
not fit well with a simplistic desire to give contemporary
parliamentary democracy deep foundations – but they have
tremendous potential as part of an analysis of how political
mechanisms evolve and mutate. In a period and globalized
setting in which parliamentary democracy no longer looks
quite as stable, all-embracing or self-evidently and automatically desirable to all, an enriched sense of the medieval contexts from which it emerged may once again become more
important to modern analysts. A similar argument could
be made regarding the idea of 'nationhood' – the roots of
which, for most European countries, undoubtedly stretch
back to the middle ages, but the sense and effect of which

have changed considerably over those centuries (as discussed in the previous chapter).[4]

In thinking about 'origins' or 'roots' and so forth, medievalists can also remind contemporary debates about less well-recognized medieval elements to modern identities. As noted in the previous chapter, work on late medieval Spain and Italy has suggested that important elements in the creation of modern ideologies of race, and associated prejudice, are located in our period, in ideas about blood lineage and 'purity', and in languages of social exclusion; more recently, literary scholars have emphasized how much, by the late middle ages, valuations of 'black' and 'white' start to function as wider social markers, providing at the very least some earlier 'sediments' (as Sara Ahmed has termed it) for modern racism.[5] There is also the concept of Europe itself, a rather obviously unstable identity in the early twenty-first century, but one that, through the shift of various global currents, has begun to rediscover the extent to which it has been unthinkingly built on a medieval notion of 'Christendom', and indeed a papal Christendom that divided the continent into 'West' and 'East'. In the multicultural and multifaith twenty-first century, medievalists have important work to do in reconsidering the ways in which Catholic Europe was constructed during the medieval centuries, the interface between individual faith and social collectivities negotiated in the process, and the relationships made and broken between political and religious power. Modern discussions about the role of faith (of whatever creed) within society have thus far been founded on a fairly unquestioned narrative of western Christian developments, in which the medieval once again plays the role of a simpler, 'pre-modern', space from which later complexities evolved. A return to the religious history of the period is likely to raise considerable questions in these areas, about the supposed unity of the Christian community, the balance of 'top-down' imposition to 'bottom-up' enthusiasm, and the very issue of what 'belief' and 'faith' are, sociologically, philosophically and politically.

The otherness or alterity of the middle ages can also be a powerful intellectual resource, not as a grotesque 'Other' to modernity, but as a reminder that how we are now is not how we have always been – and indeed that any assumed 'we' is the product of particular rather than universal circumstances. The lived contours of human experience are a fertile field here. One might think of the varying shape of medieval households: their understanding of *familia* as something extending beyond blood kin, the period of service undertaken by a large proportion of young medieval people (sometimes into their twenties) particularly in northern Europe, the different and largely less private geographies of space within domestic dwellings, and their accompanying effects on emotional, social and cultural relations. Marriage – sacralized by the Church across the high middle ages – may continue to present a link between medieval and modern, but a medieval perspective can highlight the considerable variations of practice within Europe (as discussed in Chapter 4 above). Reflection upon monasticism, chivalric association, guild membership and the like also reminds a modern audience that marriage is but one form of emotionally affective association, and was certainly not considered the 'foundation' of medieval society that some have claimed it to be for the modern era. Work on medieval gender and sexuality presents further differences. Expectations of manhood differed in important respects across social strata, and a paradox yet to be fully explored is that most medieval discussions of social roles were written by clerical men disbarred (in theory at least) from adopting lay models of full adult masculinity (combat, procreation and being head of household). Medieval notions of what constituted 'right' and 'wrong' sexual behaviour also do not map neatly onto modern expectations, the most obvious example being *sodomia*. It may not have been until the twelfth century that the sin of Sodom was understood primarily as a sexual sin; and even thereafter, *sodomia* could be defined as sexual activity that could not lead to procreation, and thus a category that potentially incorporated such 'unnatural' practices as a woman straddling a man during sex. Most importantly, it was seen as a sin – an act, to which all but the most saintly were in theory liable – rather than as part of a psychological or sociobiological identity. Modern scholarship has much debated whether or not something like a gay identity existed in the medieval period; there is little doubt, regardless of the answer, that such an identity was not identical to modern sexual identities.

In all of the above, I have implicitly been suggesting that medieval history matters if for no other reason than that it is 'good to think with'. The weakness of such an argument is that equally good claims could of course be made for other areas or disciplines. But a further support to the continued importance of medievalism is that not only is it good to think with, it has been good to think with – that is, it has been implicated, explicitly or tacitly, in various important intellectual arenas. At the broadest level, this is obviously the case with the medieval-as-antimodern arguments discussed above; to put it another way, conceptions of modernity rest upon notions of the medieval, and discussions about modernity and, indeed, postmodernity cannot escape some sense of where they are understood to have come from. Current political arguments – about ethnicity, about Islam and the West, about immigration, about globalization – frequently draw upon received narratives of western 'development' underpinned by notions of medieval-to-modern transitions. Suggestions, for example, that 'the problem' with Islam is that 'it needs a Renaissance and an Enlightenment' construct that religion as following an identical timeline to western Europe, only somehow retrograde by several centuries; and such arguments tacitly rest upon a notion that 'the problem' with medieval Christianity was somehow 'solved' by processes of Reformation and the Enlightenment.[6] Even more hatefully, we have recently seen a return to political fantasies of a racially 'pure', 'white' medieval Europe, a distortion of the complexity of ethnicities and disregard for the interconnectedness of the middle ages that appears sometimes to be spilling out from neo-Nazi websites and social media platforms to a wider rightwing audience, particularly, but not only, in the US.[7] In addressing the multiple misconceptions here implied, medievalists have an essential role before them.

Moreover, medieval studies has played a part, not always recognized by its own practitioners, in wider academic debates. Historians' analyses of serfdom, slavery and other socioeconomic factors in medieval Europe were of supreme importance to the Indian 'Subaltern Studies' group, whose work laid the foundations for postcolonial theory. Bruce Holsinger has argued that various French theorists, from Georges Bataille to Jacques Derrida to Pierre Bourdieu, made considerable use of medievalisms and have drawn ideas and language from the period itself.[8] To this particular pantheon, one could add other writers who seek to provide depth to their analyses by drawing on medieval examples, or exploring developments from the medieval to the modern, such as the anthropologist and political theorist James C. Scott and the philosopher Charles Taylor; and, of course, one may remember the importance of the medieval to the theories of Norbert Elias, Karl Marx and others.[9] These examples are worth listing not simply to cheer up those medievalists who may feel their area is underappreciated; rather, they may prompt us to recognize that medieval history is, whether it wishes it or not, in dialogue with other parts of academic and intellectual endeavour. It can remain a largely passive partner, or choose to be an active player, finding a voice with which to speak back to these other disciplinary perspectives. In order so to do, we could remember that historians are well equipped to analyse change over time, and medievalists, perhaps more than most, are accustomed to thinking of time in *la longue durée*, and of change in profound terms. Our experience of a society that is not modern – nor simply 'antimodern' – provides a powerful position from which to engage and critique more narrowly focused perspectives; and, as suggested in the previous chapter, equips medievalists well to contribute to current methodological debates in the wider field of global history.

The question of how to justify doing medieval history – or equally, why one personally wishes to pursue it – leads to a further question: what is the medieval history being done? I have discussed in the preceding chapters various and specific ways in which medieval history was, is and can be done, but the topic is worth some broader reflection in conclusion. Academic medieval history began, we might say, by providing nation-states with narratives of becoming – as both the 'roots' of their later flowering and the inchoate, pre-modern 'other' to which they gave order and meaning. In the mid-twentieth century, there was a greater focus on the creation of social structures: cities, aristocracies, hierarchical divisions that foreshadowed the wounds of 'class', and would become swept away in 1789 (from a francophone perspective) or left behind as the first western feet touched Plymouth Rock (from an American viewpoint). In recent decades, there has been a focus on the medieval as the Other of the individual modern subject – the sense of self, of identity, of what an earlier age would call 'human nature' – played out with a greater, devoutly postmodern suspicion of 'now' rather than 'then'; a delirious middle ages of alternative possibilities.

So where now? The last few sentences, my tongue partly in cheek, suggest a shifting *Zeitgeist* underlying and directing our academic endeavours; and if so, our future medieval-ist projects will presumably bring the idea of nationhood ever further under question, will interrogate the relationship between religion and society from ever more fraught view-points, and may look to medieval concepts of the common good and corporate entities as an alternative ground for political action in these globalized, post-democratic times. Less abstractly and fancifully, one can point to plenty of areas where discussion has only just begun, which must surely provide future fertile ground for research: for example, the possibilities of properly comparative history, comparative by country within the period (religious experience in pre-Reformation France and England, for example), comparative by time across the period (bureaucracies of power, 800–1400, for instance), comparative across the assumed chronological boundaries of the period (local, civic capitalisms, 1200–1700, perhaps), and comparative across wider geographical terrains (such as attempts to manage and control the natural environ-ment, from Song China to the English coast).[10] As we have seen in Chapter 3, new scientific tools are changing the ways in which we can analyse past materials and peoples, and open up fresh aspects of how medieval historians can contribute to the analysis of climate change. In literary studies, computer-assisted analysis has recently come back into play, facilitating new approaches to large textual data sets; historians may find themselves following suit, and may be either delighted or deeply unnerved by recent advances in machine-learning and manuscript palaeography.[11] The further possibilities of GIS (geographic information system) in regard to historical data, of contextually smart databases, and surely much else, all lie before us.[12] Furthermore, developments elsewhere in histori-ography will likely have some medievalist impact – as noted in Chapter 4 in the section on globalism.[13] And finally, while modern historians often seem reluctant to stray far beyond their given decade, medievalists are used to the challenge of tackling large vistas of time and space, and negotiating the demands of evidence produced by people from very different contexts and cultures. Our core topics may not, at any given moment, seem as self-evidently 'relevant' as, say, another fat book about the Nazis. But our potential ability to work and think comparatively, diachronically and with a strong sense of the protean nature of human existence makes medievalists particularly suited to framing much larger debates about the nature of history and all it contains. We are, in other words, well equipped for historiography carried out under the shadows of globalization and postmodernity.

One could also pursue the issue of 'where next?' via a methodological emphasis. Medieval history – medieval studies one might as well write – has become ever more interdisciplinary. Its practitioners periodically fret about what 'interdisciplinarity' might mean, but, in aggregate, work across and between disciplines, and informed by wider debates in the humanities and social sciences, is where the current flows. An essential demand of interdisciplinary study is that one pays attention to, and joins in with, discussion that extends beyond one's particular area of specialization. It encourages us to talk and, just as importantly, to listen. One outcome of an interdisciplinary middle ages therefore may be the greater willingness for medievalists to 'talk back', to other disciplines, to critical theory, to political debate, to the public. Our future medievalisms, one hopes, will thus be situated within wider discussions, feeding dynamically into the large, collective endeavour of the humanities.[14]

If at points medievalism has seemed 'irrelevant' to a wider readership, that is not entirely the fault of that audience, nor the shifting currents of the contemporary *Zeitgeist*, but also the attitudes of a few past practitioners, who at various points were happy to rest on nineteenth-century laurels and smugly ignore the changing world – and then retreat wistfully into the imagined lands of their period as the climate around them grew less welcoming. 'We should never forget our greatest danger: we began as antiquarians and we could end as antiquarians', as Joseph Strayer remarked in 1971.[15] This may seem pessimistic, but is in fact quite the opposite.

Those days are largely gone. Medieval studies today is an area of discussion, debate and passionate argument, prompted and encouraged by the communicative demands of interdisciplinarity, set within an avowedly international frame. Those whose formative academic years are being shaped by such dialectics are well equipped not only to pursue the ongoing discussion within the discipline, but also to carry the debate further afield, to pastures new.

Notes

Chapter 1   Framing the Middle Ages

1   It is possible (if *mapellus* is a variant or mistranscription of *napellus*) that this was a juice made from the plant monkshood (aconite); my thanks to Richard Kieckhefer.
2   Bartolomeo's depositions are edited from the Vatican archives in P. K. Eubel, 'Vom Zaubereiunwesen anfangs des 14. Jahrhunderts', *Historisches Jahrbuch* 18 (1897): 609–25. The case is discussed, and further evidence against the Visconti edited from MS Vat. Lat. 3936, in R. Michel, 'Le procès de Matteo et de Galeazzo Visconti', *Mélanges d'archéologie et d'histoire de l'École Française de Rome* 29 (1909): 269–327.
3   U. Eco, 'Dreaming of the Middle Ages', in *Travels in Hyperreality* (London, 1987), 69.
4   Quoted in E. Breisach, *Historiography: Ancient, Medieval and Modern* (Chicago, 1983), 207.
5   P. Burke, 'Ranke the Reactionary', *Syracuse Scholar* 9 (1988): 25–30; A. Grafton, *The Footnote: A Curious History* (London, 1997).
6   P. Novick, *That Noble Dream: The Objectivity Question and the American Historical Profession* (Cambridge, 1988), 26–30.
7   M. Innes, 'A Fatal Disjuncture? Medieval History and Medievalism in the UK', in H.-W. Goetz and J. Jarnut, eds, *Mediävistik im 21. Jahrhundert* (Munich, 2003), 73–100; R. N. Soffer, *Discipline and Power: The University, History, and the Making of an English Elite 1870–1930* (Stanford, 1994).
8   C. Carpenter, 'Political and Constitutional History', in R. H.

Britnell and A. J. Pollard, eds, *The McFarlane Legacy* (Stroud, 1995), 175–206.

9   M. Bloch, *La Société féodale*, 2 vols (Paris, 1939, 1940); *Feudal Society*, trans. L. A. Manyon (London, 1961). M. Bloch, *Apologie pour l'histoire, ou Métier d'historien* (Paris, 1949); *The Historian's Craft*, trans. P. Putnam (New York, 1953).

10 H. J. Kaye, *The British Marxist Historians*, 2nd edn (Basingstoke, 1995).

11 Novick, *That Noble Dream*; P. Freedman and G. Spiegel, 'Medievalisms Old and New', *American Historical Review* 103 (1998): 677–704.

12 G. Spiegel, 'History, Historicism, and the Social Logic of the Text in the Middle Ages', *Speculum* 65 (1990): 59–68; P. Zumthor, *Speaking of the Middle Ages*, trans. S. White (Lincoln, NB, 1986).

13 W. R. Keylor, *Academy and Community: The Establishment of the French Historical Profession* (Cambridge, MA, 1975), 43ff.

14 N. F. Cantor, *Inventing the Middle Ages* (Cambridge, 1991), 86ff. Cantor's book must be treated cautiously on this and other topics – see the review by Robert Bartlett, *New York Review of Books* 39.9 (14 May 1992) and subsequent discussion (*NYRB* 39.14) – but it raises important issues nonetheless. On Kantorowicz, see the marvellous R. E. Lerner, *Ernst Kantorowicz: A Life* (Princeton, 2017).

15 S. Berger, M. Donovan and K. Passmore, eds, *Writing National Histories* (London, 1999).

16 E. Power, *The Goodman of Paris* (London, 1928); *Le Menagier de Paris*, ed. G. E. Brereton and J. M. Ferrier (Oxford, 1981).

Chapter 2   Tracing the Middle Ages

1   *Anonimalle Chronicle, 1333 to 1381*, ed. V. H. Galbraith (Manchester, 1927), 151.

2   C. Dyer, 'The Rising of 1381 in Suffolk', in *Everyday Life in Medieval England* (London, 2000), 221–40; H. Eiden, 'Joint Action Against "Bad" Lordship: The Peasants' Revolt in Essex and Norfolk', *History* 83 (1998): 5–30.

3   J. G. Clark, 'Thomas Walsingham Reconsidered', *Speculum* 77 (2002): 832–60.

4   For example, David d'Avray's discussion of editing sermons in his *Medieval Marriage Sermons* (Oxford, 2001).

5   R. H. Bloch, *God's Plagiarist* (Chicago, 1995).
6   R. Brentano, *A New World in a Small Place: Church and Religion in the Diocese of Rieti, 1188–1378* (Berkeley, 1994).
7   There is also a National Library in Florence, which contains some medieval manuscripts, though considerably more limited than its French or English equivalents.
8   R. F. Berkhofer, *Day of Reckoning: Power and Accountability in Medieval France* (Philadelphia, 2004).
9   S. D. Goitein, *A Mediterranean Society* (Berkeley, 1967–93), 6 vols.
10 For a thorough guide, see J. A. Burrow and T. Turville-Peter, eds, *A Book of Middle English* (Oxford, 1991).
11 H. Tsurushima, ed., *Haskins Society Journal, Japan* 1 (2005).
12 Patrologia Latina 198, 441–2, quoted in C. Holdsworth, 'Were the Sermons of St Bernard on the Song of Songs ever Preached?', in C. Muessig, ed., *Medieval Monastic Sermons* (Leiden, 1998), 295.
13 Robert Mannyng of Brunne, *Handlyng Synne*, ed. I. Sullens (Binghamton, 1983), 225–31.
14 R. McKitterick, 'Political Ideology in Carolingian Historiography', in Y. Hen and M. Innes, eds, *The Uses of the Past in the Early Middle Ages* (Cambridge, 2000), 162–74.
15 P. E. Dutton, 'Raoul Glaber's "De Divina Quaternitate"', *Mediaeval Studies* 42 (1980): 431–53; F. Ortigues and D. Iogna-Prat, 'Raoul Glaber et l'historiographie clunisienne', *Studi Medievali* 26.2 (1985): 537–72.
16 Rodolphus Glaber, *Historiarum libri quinque*, ed. and trans. J. France (Oxford, 1989), 94–5 (III, i).
17 Dino Compagni, *Chronicle of Florence*, trans. D. E. Bornstein (Philadelphia, 1986).
18 G. M. Spiegel, *Romancing the Past: The Rise of Vernacular Prose Historiography in Thirteenth-Century France* (Berkeley, 1993), 2.
19 *The Chronicle of San Juan de la Peña*, trans. L. H. Nelson (Philadelphia, 1991).
20 *Annales Erfordienses*, Monumenta Germaniae Historica, Scriptores 16, 29.
21 Richer of Saint-Rémi, *Histories*, ed. and trans. J. Lake, 2 vols (Cambridge, MA, 2011), II, p. 307 (Bk IV, cap. 50).
22 K. Şahin, 'Constantinople and the End Time: The Ottoman Conquest as a Portent of the Last Hour', *Journal of Early Modern History* 14.4 (2010): 317–54.
23 R. W. Southern, 'Aspects of the European Tradition of Historical Writing' I–IV, *Transactions of the Royal Historical*

Society [hereafter *TRHS*], 5th series, 20–3 (1970–3); Jean de
Joinville, *Life of Saint Louis, in Joinville and Villehardouin:
Chronicles of the Crusades*, trans. M. R. B. Shaw (London,
1963).

24   S. Bagge, *Kings, Politics and the Right Order of the World in
German Historiography c.950–1150* (Leiden, 2002).

25   S. Justice, *Writing and Rebellion: England in 1381* (Princeton,
1994).

26   E. van Houts, *Memory and Gender in Medieval Europe, 900–
1200* (Houndmills, 1999).

27   W. Davies, 'People and places in dispute in ninth-century
Brittany', in W. Davies and P. Fouracre, eds, *The Settlement of
Disputes in Early Medieval Europe* (Cambridge, 1986), 75.

28   A more precise and technical set of definitions for charters,
chirographs and other English documents is given in M. T.
Clanchy, *From Memory to Written Record*, 2nd edn (Oxford,
1993), 85–92.

29   P. Górecki, *Economy, Society and Lordship in Medieval
Poland, 1100–1250* (New York, 1992), 51.

30   A. J. Kosto, 'Laymen, Clerics and Documentary Practices in the
Early Middle Ages', *Speculum* 80 (2005): 44.

31   Kosto, 'Laymen'; W. C. Brown, 'When Documents are
Destroyed or Lost', *Early Medieval Europe* 11 (2002): 337–66;
W. C. Brown, M. Costambeys, M. Innes and A. J. Kosto, eds,
Documentary Culture and the Laity in the Early Middle Ages
(Cambridge, 2013).

32   Clanchy, *From Memory to Written Record*, 46ff.

33   R. C. van Caenegem, *Guide to the Sources of Medieval History*
(Amsterdam, 1978), 72.

34   B. Rosenwein, *To Be the Neighbour of St Peter: The Social
Meaning of Cluny's Property, 909–1049* (Ithaca, 1989).

35   B. Bedos-Rezak, 'Civic Liturgies and Urban Records in Northern
France 1100–1400', in B. A. Hanawalt and K. L. Reyerson,
eds, *City and Spectacle in Medieval Europe* (Minneapolis,
1994), 34–55.

36   For one sense of this, see W. Brown, 'Charters as Weapons',
Journal of Medieval History 28 (2002): 227–48.

37   D. Alexandre-Bidou, 'Une foi en deux ou trois dimensions?',
Annales: Histoire, Sciences Sociales 53.6 (1998): 1155–90.

38   J.-C. Schmitt, 'Images and the Historian', in A. Bolvig and
P. Lindley, eds, *History and Images* (Turnhout, 2003), 19–44;
and, more broadly, J. Baschet and J.-C. Schmitt, eds, *L'Image*
(Paris, 1996).

39   M. Pastoureau, 'Voir les couleurs du Moyen Age', in *Une*

histoire symbolique du Moyen Age occidental (Paris, 2004), 113–33.

40 For example, F. Garnier, *Le Langage de l'image au Moyen Age*, 2 vols (Paris, 1982–9).

41 Personal visit by the author to the church. Some images, including this one, can be seen at www.kalkmalerier.dk.

42 M. Kupfer, *Romanesque Wall Painting in Central France* (New Haven, 1993).

43 E. Welch, *Art and Society in Italy, 1350–1500* (Oxford, 1997), 295–302, figs 152, 153.

44 J. Alexander, 'Labour and Paresse: Ideological Representations of Medieval Peasant Labour', *Art Bulletin* 72 (1990): 436–52.

45 D. H. Strickland, *Saracens, Demons and Jews* (Princeton, 2003); S. Lipton, *Dark Mirror: The Medieval Origins of Anti-Jewish Iconography* (New York, 2014).

46 N. Rubinstein, 'Political Ideas in Sienese Art', *Journal of the Warburg and Courtauld Institutes* 21 (1958): 179–207.

47 S. Y. Edgerton Jr, *Pictures and Punishment* (Ithaca, 1985).

48 D. O. Hughes, 'Representing the Family', *Journal of Interdisciplinary History* 17 (1986): 13–14.

49 S. Lipton, '"The Sweet Lean of His Head"', *Speculum* 80 (2005): 1172–208.

50 M. Camille, 'At the Sign of the Spinning Sow', in Bolvig and Lindley, eds, *History and Images*, 249–76.

51 M. B. Merback, *The Thief, the Cross and the Wheel: Pain and the Spectacle of Punishment in Medieval and Renaissance Europe* (Chicago, 1998), 124–5.

52 H. C. Lea, *A History of Inquisition in the Middle Ages* (New York, 1888), I, iii–iv.

53 *The Code of Cuenca*, trans. J. F. Powers (Philadelphia, 2000), 91.

54 S. Reynolds, *Kingdoms and Communities in Western Europe, 900–1300* (Oxford, 1984), 268–71.

55 P. J. P. Goldberg, ed., *Women in England, 1275–1525* (Manchester, 1995), 239.

56 G. Ruggiero, *The Boundaries of Eros: Sex, Crime and Sexuality in Renaissance Venice* (Oxford, 1985).

57 T. Dean, *Crime in Medieval Europe* (Harlow, 2001), 77–8.

58 B. Hanawalt, *The Ties that Bound: Peasant Families in Medieval England* (Oxford, 1986); S. Farmer, *Surviving Poverty in Medieval Paris* (Ithaca, 2002); C. Gauvard, *De Grace Especial*, 2 vols (Paris, 1991); E. Le Roy Ladurie, *Montaillou* (Paris, 1978).

59 D. L. Smail, *The Consumption of Justice: Emotions, Publicity*

and Legal Culture in Marseille, 1264–1423 (Ithaca, 2003); A. Musson, ed., *Expectations of the Law in the Middle Ages* (Woodbridge, 2001).
60   J. Duvernoy, ed., *L'Inquisition en Quercy* (Castelnaud La Chapelle, 2001), 148.
61   D. L. Smail, 'Common Violence: Vengeance and Inquisition in Fourteenth-Century Marseille', *Past & Present* 151 (1996): 55–7.
62   C. Wickham, *Courts and Conflict in Twelfth-Century Tuscany* (Oxford, 2003); P. Hyams, *Rancor and Reconciliation in Medieval England* (Ithaca, 2003).
63   J. B. Given, *Inquisition and Medieval Society* (Ithaca, 1998); J. H. Arnold, *Inquisition and Power* (Philadelphia, 2001).

Chapter 3   Reading the Middle Ages

1   Ramon Muntaner, *The Chronicle of Muntaner*, trans. Lady Goodenough, Hakluyt Society, 2nd series 47, 50 (reprint: Nendeln, 1967), I, 10–16 (cap. III–VI).
2   R. C. Rhodes, 'Emile Durkheim and the Historical Thought of Marc Bloch', *Theory and Society* 5 (1978): 45–73; P. Burke, *The French Historical Revolution: The Annales School 1929–89* (Cambridge, 1990), 16ff.
3   For example, E. Cohen and M. de Jong, eds, *Medieval Transformations: Texts, Power and the Gift in Context* (Leiden, 2001); W. I. Miller, 'Gift, Sale, Payment, Raid: Case Studies in the Negotiation and Classification of Exchange in Medieval Iceland', *Speculum* 61 (1986): 18–50; M. de Jong, *In Samuel's Image: Child Oblation in the Early Middle Ages* (Leiden, 1994).
4   J. Le Goff, *Time, Work and Culture in the Middle Ages* (Chicago, 1980) and *The Medieval Imagination* (Chicago, 1985).
5   V. Turner, *The Ritual Process* (Chicago, 1969).
6   C. Walker Bynum, 'Women's Stories, Women's Symbols', in *Fragmentation and Redemption* (New York, 1991), 27–51.
7   P. Brown, 'The Rise and Function of the Holy Man in Late Antiquity', in *Society and the Holy in Late Antiquity* (London, 1982), 103–52; P. Brown, 'The Christian Holy Man in Late Antiquity', in *Authority and the Sacred* (Cambridge, 1995), 55–78.
8   J. Goody and I. Watt, 'The Consequences of Literacy', in J. Goody, ed., *Literacy in Traditional Societies* (Cambridge,

1968), 27–68; W. Ong, *Orality and Literacy* (London, 1982).

9   J. M. H. Smith, *Europe After Rome: A New Cultural History 500–1000* (Oxford, 2005), 38–9.

10   J. Halverson, 'Goody and the Implosion of the Literacy Thesis', *Man* n.s. 27 (1992): 301–17.

11   B. Stock, *The Implications of Literacy* (Princeton, 1983).

12   P. Bourdieu, *Outline of a Theory of Practice* (Cambridge, 1977); M. de Certeau, *The Practice of Everyday Life* (Berkeley, 1984).

13   T. Fenster and D. L. Smail, eds, *Fama: The Politics of Talk and Reputation in Medieval Europe* (Ithaca, 2003); C. Wickham, 'Gossip and Resistance among the Medieval Peasantry', *Past & Present* 160 (1998): 3–24.

14   W. I. Miller, *Bloodtaking and Peacemaking: Feud, Law and Society in Saga Iceland* (Chicago, 1990).

15   See http://www.stg.brown.edu/projects/catasto/overview.html. Note that one must read all the accompanying files, particularly the 'code book', in order to make meaningful use of the database. The source is described in further detail in *Les Toscans et leurs familles*, and more briefly in the English translation: *Tuscans and Their Families* (New Haven, 1985).

16   S. K. Cohn, 'Prosperity in the Countryside', in *Women in the Streets* (Baltimore, 1996), 137–65.

17   S. K. Cohn, *The Cult of Remembrance and the Black Death* (Baltimore, 1992).

18   S. A. C. Penn and C. Dyer, 'Wages and Earnings in Late Medieval England', *Economic History Review* n.s. 43 (1990): 356–76.

19   H. Swanson, 'The Illusion of Economic Structure', *Past & Present* 121 (1988): 29–48; G. Rosser, 'Crafts, Guilds and the Negotiation of Work in the Medieval Town', *Past & Present* 154 (1997): 3–31.

20   J. M. Murray, *Bruges, Cradle of Capitalism 1280–1390* (Cambridge, 2005), 130ff.

21   J. Davis, 'Baking for the Common Good', *Economic History Review* n.s. 57 (2004): 465–502.

22   For a recent picture of a Marxist middle ages, with critical commentary, see S. H. Rigby, 'Historical Materialism: Social Structure and Social Change in the Middle Ages', *Journal of Medieval and Early Modern Studies* 34 (2004): 473–522.

23   C. Dyer, *An Age of Transition? Economy and Society in England in the Later Middle Ages* (Oxford, 2005).

24   For what follows, see I. Biron et al., 'Techniques and Materials

in Limoges Enamels', in J. P. O'Neil, ed., *Enamels of Limoges, 1100–1350* (New York, 1996).

25   For a recent view on past legacies and current possibilities, see L. Bourgeois, et al., eds, *La Culture matérielle: Un objet en question. Anthropologie, archéologie et histoire. Actes du colloque international de Caen (9 et 10 octobre 2015)* (Caen, 2018).

26   B. K. Davison, 'The Origins of the Castle in England', *Archaeological Journal* 124 (1967): 202–11; R. Allen Brown, 'An Historian's Approach to the Origins of the Castle in England', *Archaeological Journal* 126 (1969): 131–48; R. Liddiard, ed., *Anglo-Norman Castles* (Woodbridge, 2003).

27   R. Liddiard, *Castles in Context* (Macclesfield, 2005).

28   A. I. Beach, *Women as Scribes: Book Production and Monastic Reform in Twelfth-Century Bavaria* (Cambridge, 2004); A. Radini et al., 'Medieval Women's Early Involvement in Manuscript Production Suggested by Lapis Lazuli Identification in Dental Calculus', *Science Advances* 5 (2019).

29   R. Gilchrist and B. Sloane, *Requiem: The Medieval Monastic Cemetery in Britain* (London, 2005).

30   V. Thompson, *Death and Dying in Later Anglo-Saxon England* (Woodbridge, 2004), 33–5.

31   B. Effros, *Caring for Body and Soul* (University Park, PA, 2002) and *Merovingian Mortuary Archaeology* (Berkeley, 2003). See also H. Williams, 'Rethinking Early Medieval Mortuary Archaeology', *Early Medieval Europe* 13 (2005): 195–217.

32   F. Curta, *The Making of the Slavs* (Cambridge, 2005).

33   A. M. Koldeweij, 'Lifting the Veil on Pilgrim Badges', in J. Stopford, ed., *Pilgrimage Explored* (York, 1999), 161–88.

34   T. Williamson, *Shaping Medieval Landscapes* (Macclesfield, 2002).

35   P. Sawyer, 'Markets and Fairs in Norway and Sweden between the Eighth and Sixteenth Centuries', in T. Pestell and K. Ulmscheider, eds, *Markets in Early Medieval Europe* (Macclesfield, 2003), 168–74.

36   H. Pirenne, *Mahomet et Charlemagne* (Brussels, 1937).

37   M. McCormick, *Origins of the European Economy* (Cambridge, 2001).

38   S. Fiddyment, et al., 'So You Want to Do Biocodicology? A Field Guide to the Biological Analysis of Parchment', *Heritage Science* 7 (2019): 1–10.

39   K. R. Dark, 'Houses, Streets and Shops in Byzantine Constantinople from the Fifth to the Twelfth Centuries', *Journal of Medieval History* 30 (2004): 83–107.

40 R. Gilchrist and M. Oliva, *Religious Women in Medieval East Anglia* (Norwich, 1993); R. Gilchrist, *Gender and Material Culture* (London, 1994), 163–7.

41 J. Masschaele, 'The Public Space of the Marketplace in Medieval England', *Speculum* 77 (2002): 383–421; D. C. Mengel, 'From Venice to Jerusalem and Beyond: Milíč of Kroměříz and the Topography of Prostitution in Fourteenth-Century Prague', *Speculum* 79 (2004): 407–42.

42 For an early example, see C. Pamela Graves, 'Social Space in the English Medieval Parish Church', *Economy and Society* 18 (1989): 297–322.

43 D. Raoult, et al., 'Molecular Identification by "Suicide PCR" of *Yersinia pestis* as the Agent of Medieval Black Death', *Proceedings of the National Academy of Sciences* 97.23 (2000); S. Haensch et al., 'Distinct Clones of *Yersinia Pestis* Caused the Black Death', *PLOS Pathogens* 6 (2010); K. I. Bos, et al., 'A Draft Genome of *Yersinia pestis* from Victims of the Black Death', *Nature* 478 (2011); L. Seifert, et al., 'Strategy for Sensitive and Specific Detection of *Yersinia pestis* in Skeletons of the Black Death Pandemic', *PLOS One* 8.9 (2013).

44 Y. Cui et al., 'Historical Variations in Mutation Rate in an Epidemic Pathogen, *Yersinia pestis*', *Proceedings of the National Academy of Sciences of the USA* 110 (2013); D. M. Wagner et al., '*Yersinia pestis* and the Plague of Justinian 541–543 AD: A Genomic Analysis', *The Lancet: Infectious Diseases* 14.4 (2014); M. Feldman et al., 'A High-Coverage *Yersinia pestis* Genome from a Sixth-Century Justinianic Plague Victim', *Molecular Biology and Evolution* 33.11 (2016).

45 M. H. Green, 'Taking "Pandemic" Seriously: Making the Black Death Global', in M. H. Green, ed., *Pandemic Disease in the Medieval World* (Kalamazoo, 2015); M. H. Green, 'Putting Africa on the Black Death Map: Narratives from Genetics and History', *Afriques* 9 (2018).

46 P. J. Geary, 'The Use of Ancient DNA to Analyze Population Movements between Pannonia and Italy in the Sixth Century', in *Le migrazioni nell'alto medioevo, Settimane di Studio LXVI* (Spoleto, 2019); P. J. Geary, et al., 'Understanding 6th-century Barbarian Social Organization and Migration through Paleogenomics', *Nature Communications* 9 (2018); P. J. Geary, et al., 'A Genetic Perspective on Longobard Era Migrations', *European Journal of Human Genetics* 27 (2019).

47 L.-J. Richardson and T. Booth, 'Response to "Brexit, Archaeology and Heritage: Reflections and Agendas"', *Papers from the Institute of Archaeology* 27.1 (2017).

48   F. C. Ljungqvist, 'A New Reconstruction of Temperature Variability in the Extra-Tropical Northern Hemisphere During the Last Two Millennia', *Physical Geography* 92.3 (2010): 339–51; J. Servonnat et al., 'Influence of Solar Variability, CO_2 and Orbital Forcing between 1000 and 1850 AD in the IPSLCM4 Model', *Climate Past* 6 (2010): 445–60.

49   B. M. S. Campbell, *The Great Transition: Climate, Disease and Society in the Late Medieval World* (Cambridge, 2016). For an important review and context, see M. Green, 'Black as Death', *Inference: International Review of Science* 4 (2018).

50   K. Pribyl, *Farming, Famine and Plague: The Impact of Climate in Late Medieval England* (Cham, 2017).

51   S. Helama et al., 'Something Old, Something New, Something Borrowed: New Insights to Human–Environment Interaction in Medieval Novgorod Inferred from Tree Rings', *Journal of Archaeological Science: Reports* 13 (2017); U. Büntgen and N. di Cosmo, 'Climatic and Environmental Aspects of the Mongol Withdrawal from Hungary in 1242 CE', *Scientific Reports* 6 (2016); see rejoinder by Pinke et al., and further response by Büntgen and di Cosmo, in the two subsequent issues.

52   See the warnings in P. Squatriti, 'The Floods of 589 and Climate Change at the Beginning of the Middle Ages: An Italian Microhistory', *Speculum* 85 (2010); note also broader caveats in R. Hoffmann, *An Environmental History of Medieval Europe* (Cambridge, 2014), Ch. 9.

53   Edited in A. Flores, *Mediaeval Age* (London, 1963), 141; the translation (by Gillian Barker and Kenneth Gee) slightly amended here, with thanks to Professor David Wells.

54   R. M. Karras, *From Boys to Men* (Philadelphia, 2002).

55   J. Watts, 'The Pressure of the Public on Later Medieval Politics', in L. Clark and C. Carpenter, eds, *Political Culture in Late Medieval Britain* (Woodbridge, 2004), 159–80.

56   W. M. Ormrod, 'The Use of English: Language, Law and Political Culture in Fourteenth-Century England', *Speculum* 78 (2003): 750–87.

57   C. Brémond, J. Le Goff and J.-C. Schmitt, *L'Exemplum* (Turnhout, 1982), 111–43; J. H. Arnold, 'The Labour of Continence', in A. Bernau, R. Evans and S. Salih, eds, *Medieval Virginities* (Cardiff, 2003), 102–18.

58   B. Hanawalt, 'Whose Story Was This? Rape Narratives in Medieval English Courts', in *Of Good and Ill Repute: Gender and Social Control in Medieval England* (Oxford, 1998), 124–41.

59 M. Toch, 'Asking the Way and Telling the Law: Speech in Medieval Germany', *Journal of Interdisciplinary History* 16 (1986): 667–82.

60 For example, J. Dumolyn and J. Haemers, '"A Bad Chicken Was Brooding": Subversive Speech in Late Medieval Flanders', *Past & Present* 214 (2012); C. D. Liddy, *Contesting the City: The Politics of Citizenship in English Towns, 1250–1530* (Oxford, 2017); T. Dutour, *Sous l'Empire du bien: 'Bonnes gens' et pacte social (XIIIe–XVe siècles)* (Paris, 2015).

61 C. Clover, '"Regardless of Sex": Men, Women and Power in Early Northern Europe', *Speculum* 68 (1993): 363–87; R. N. Swanson, 'Angels Incarnate?', in D. Hadley, ed., *Masculinity in Medieval Europe* (Harlow, 1999), 160–77.

62 J. Burckhardt, *The Civilisation of the Renaissance in Italy* (London, 1860).

63 R. W. Southern, *The Making of the Middle Ages* (London, 1953); W. Ullmann, *The Individual and Society in the Middle Ages* (Baltimore, 1966); C. Morris, *The Discovery of the Individual 1050–1200* (London, 1972).

64 C. W. Bynum, 'Did the Twelfth Century Discover the Individual?', in *Jesus as Mother* (Berkeley, 1982), 97.

65 R. Kaeuper, *Chivalry and Violence in Medieval Europe* (Oxford, 1999); S. Crane, *The Performance of Self: Ritual, Clothing and Identity During the Hundred Years War* (Philadelphia, 2002).

66 P. Blickle, *The Revolution of 1525* (London, 1991).

Chapter 4   Debating the Middle Ages

1 S. K. Cohn, *The Black Death Transformed* (London, 2002).

2 M. Zerner, ed., *Inventer l'hérésie?* (Nice, 1998); P. Biller, 'Goodbye to Waldensianism?', *Past & Present* 192 (2006): 3–33; F. Somerset et al., eds, *Lollards and Their Influence in Late Medieval England* (Woodbridge, 2003).

3 R. I. Moore, *Formation of a Persecuting Society* (London, 1985); see reflections in J. H. Arnold, 'Persecution and Power in Medieval Europe', *American Historical Review* 123 (2018): 165–74.

4 S. Farmer, *Surviving Poverty in Medieval Paris* (Ithaca, 2002); D. L. Smail, *Imaginary Cartographies: Possession and Identity in Late Medieval Marseille* (Ithaca, 2003); C. Beattie, *Medieval Single Women* (Oxford, 2007).

5 *The Annals of Flodoard of Reims, 919–966*, ed. S. Fanning

and B. S. Bachrach (Ontario, 2004), 10–11; see G. Koziol, *Begging Pardon and Favor: Ritual and Political Order in Early Medieval France* (Ithaca, 1992), 111.

6 R. Hutton, *The Rise and Fall of Merry England* (Oxford, 1994); R. W. Scribner, 'Ritual and Popular Religion in Catholic Germany', *Journal of Ecclesiastical History* 35 (1984): 47–77.

7 G. Althoff, *Spielregeln der Politik im Mittelalter* (Darmstadt, 1997); G. Althoff, 'The Variability of Rituals in the Middle Ages', in G. Althoff, J. Fried and P. Geary, eds, *Medieval Concepts of the Past* (Cambridge, 2001), 71–87.

8 E. Palazzo, *L'Invention chrétienne des cinq sens dans la liturgie et l'art au Moyen Age* (Paris, 2014); M. C. Gaposchkin, *Invisible Weapons: Liturgy and the Making of Crusade Ideology* (Ithaca, 2017).

9 P. Buc, *The Dangers of Ritual* (Princeton, 2001).

10 *The Ecclesiastical History of Orderic Vitalis*, ed. M. Chibnall (Oxford, 1975), V, 315–21 (bk X, cap. 19).

11 H. Fichtenau, *Living in the Tenth Century* (Chicago, 1991), 32.

12 S. Lindenbaum, 'Ceremony and Oligarchy', in Hanawalt and Reyerson, eds, *City and Spectacle*, 171–88.

13 Koziol, *Begging Pardon and Favor*, 298.

14 T. Asad, *Genealogies of Religion* (Baltimore, 1993).

15 G. Althoff, 'Ira Regis: Prolegomena to a History of Royal Anger', in B. Rosenwein, ed., *Anger's Past* (Ithaca, 1998), 59–74.

16 C. Phythian-Adams, 'Ceremony and the Citizen', in P. Clark and P. Slack, eds, *Crisis and Order in English Towns 1500–1700* (London, 1972), 57–85; J. Bossy, 'The Mass as a Social Institution 1200–1700', *Past & Present* 100 (1983): 29–61. See also M. James, 'Ritual, Drama and Social Body in the Late Medieval English Town', *Past & Present* 98 (1983): 3–29, although his analysis is more subtle than later critics sometimes credit.

17 Koziol, *Begging Pardon and Favor*; W. I. Miller, *Bloodtaking and Peacemaking: Feud, Law and Society in Saga Iceland* (Chicago, 1990); C. Wickham, *Courts and Conflict in Twelfth-Century Tuscany* (Oxford, 2003); see also W. Davies and P. Fouracre, eds, *The Settlement of Disputes in Early Medieval Europe* (Cambridge, 1986).

18 A. W. Lewis, 'Forest Rights and the Celebration of May', *Mediaeval Studies* 53 (1991): 259–77.

19 S. MacLean, 'Ritual, Misunderstanding and the Contest for

Meaning', in B. Weiler and S. MacLean, eds, *Representations of Power in Medieval Germany 800–1500* (Turnhout, 2006), 97–119.

20 K. Petkov, *The Kiss of Peace* (Leiden, 2003); K. M. Phillips, 'The Invisible Man: Body and Ritual in a Fifteenth-Century Noble Household', *Journal of Medieval History* 31 (2005): 143–62.

21 G. Duby, *La Société aux XIe et XIIe siècles dans la région Mâconnaise* (Paris, 1953).

22 S. Reynolds, *Fiefs and Vassals* (Oxford, 1994); D. Barthélemy, *La Mutation de l'an mil, a-t-elle eu lieu?* (Paris, 1997).

23 *The Usatges of Barcelona*, ed. and trans. D. J. Kagay (Philadelphia, 1991), 65–6 (nos 4–7, 9, 11).

24 Alain de Lille, *The Art of Preaching* (Kalamazoo, 1981); these being only the lay categories, with further sermons for various kinds of *oratores*.

25 R. van Uytven, 'Showing off One's Rank in the Middle Ages', in W. Blockmans and A. Janse, eds, *Showing Status: Representation of Social Positions in the Late Middle Ages* (Turnhout, 1999), 20.

26 *Usatges*, 67 (nos 8, 10).

27 Joseph Morsel argues provocatively that the concept of 'the nobility' as a group only appeared *c.*1400; 'Inventing a Social Category: The Sociogenesis of the Nobility at the End of the Middle Ages', in B. Jussen, ed., *Ordering Medieval Society* (Philadelphia, 2001), 200–40.

28 S. Imsen, 'King Magnus and Liegemen's "Hirðskrå": A Portrait of the Norwegian Nobility in the 1270s', in A. J. Duggan, ed., *Nobles and Nobility in Medieval Europe* (Woodbridge, 2000), 205–20.

29 R. Bartlett, *The Making of Europe* (London, 1993), 47.

30 M. H. Gelting, 'Legal Reform and the Development of Peasant Dependence in Thirteenth-Century Denmark', in P. Freedman and M. Bourin, eds, *Forms of Servitude in Northern and Central Europe* (Turnhout, 2005), 343–68; J. M. Bak, 'Servitude in the Medieval Kingdom of Hungary', in Freedman and Bourin, eds, *Forms of Servitude in Northern and Central Europe*, 387–400; P. Jones, 'From Manor to *mezzadria*', in N. Rubinstein, ed., *Florentine Studies* (London, 1968), 193–241.

31 P. Franklin, 'Politics in Manorial Court Rolls', in Z. Razi and R. Smith, eds, *Medieval Society and the Manor Court* (Oxford, 1996), 162–98; R. B. Goheen, 'Peasant Politics? Village Community and the Crown in Fifteenth-Century England', *American Historical Review* 96 (1991): 42–62.

32   S. Shahar, *The Fourth Estate: A History of Women in the Middle Ages* (London, 1983).
33   R. M. Smith, 'Geographical Diversity in the Resort to Marriage in Late Medieval Europe', in P. J. P. Goldberg, ed., *Women in Medieval English Society* (Stroud, 1997), 16–59.
34   A. J. Duggan, ed., *Queens and Queenship in Medieval Europe* (Woodbridge, 2002); S. J. Johns, *Noblewomen, Aristocracy and Power in the Twelfth-Century Anglo-Norman Realm* (Manchester, 2003).
35   K. Parker, 'Lynn and the Making of a Mystic', in J. H. Arnold and K. J. Lewis, eds, *A Companion to the Book of Margery Kempe* (Cambridge, 2004), 55–74.
36   William Caxton, *The Game of Chess* (London, 1870) (facs. BL King's Library C.10.b.23), second traytye, pars 11.
37   Ibn Khaldûn, *The Muqaddimah*, trans. R. Rosenthal, abridged by N. J. Dawood (Princeton, 2005), 279.
38   J. Abu-Lughod, *Before European Hegemony: The World System* AD *1250–1350* (Oxford, 1989).
39   P. Spufford, *Power and Profit: The Merchant in Medieval Europe* (London, 2002), 248–55, 309–18; P. Freedman, *Out of the East: Spice and the Medieval Imagination* (New Haven, 2008).
40   Spufford, *Power and Profit*, 311.
41   V. Hansen, *The Silk Road: A New History* (Oxford, 2012).
42   J. de Vries, 'The Limits of Globalization in the Early Modern World', *Economic History Review* 63 (2010).
43   For one key example, see most recently S. Davis-Secord, *Where Three Worlds Met: Sicily in the Early Medieval Mediterranean* (Ithaca, 2017).
44   D. Nirenberg, 'Mass Conversion and Genealogical Mentalities: Jews and Christians in Fifteenth-Century Spain', *Past & Present* 174 (2002); S. A. Epstein, *Speaking of Slavery: Color, Ethnicity and Human Bondage in Italy* (Ithaca, 2001).
45   B. Jervis, 'Assembling the Archaeology of the Global Middle Ages', *World Archaeology* 49 (2017).
46   On the latter, in part see J. Rubin, *Learning in a Crusader City: Intellectual Activity and Intercultural Exchanges in Acre, 1191–1291* (Cambridge, 2018).
47   M. A. Gomez, *African Dominion: A New History of Empire in Early and Medieval West Africa* (Princeton, 2018), 106.
48   For one such attempt, see M. S. G. Hodgson, *The Venture of Islam: Conscience and History in a World Civilization*, 3 vols (Chicago, 1974).
49   R. I. Moore, 'A Global Middle Ages?', in J. Belich, et al., eds, *The Prospect of Global History* (Oxford, 2016).

50 D. Goodall and A. Wareham, 'The Political Significance of Gifts of Power in the Khmer and Mercian Kingdoms 793–926', *Medieval Worlds* 6 (2017): 156–95 at p. 179.

51 A few indicative examples: S. Yarrow, 'Masculinity as a World Historical Category of Analysis', in J. H. Arnold and S. Brady, eds, *What Is Masculinity?* (Houndmills, 2011); R. Forster and N. Yavari, eds, *Global Medieval: Mirrors for Princes Reconsidered* (Boston, 2015); J. T. Palmer, 'The Global Eminent Life: Sixth-Century Collected Biographies from Gregory of Tours to Huijiao of Jiaxiang Temple', *Medieval Worlds* 8 (2018).

52 K. Davis, *Periodization and Sovereignty: How Ideas of Feudalism and Secularization Govern the Politics of Time* (Philadelphia, 2008); G. Heng, 'Early Globalities, and its Questions, Objectives and Methods', *Exemplaria* 26 (2014).

53 C. Holmes and N. Standen, eds, *The Global Middle Ages* (Oxford, 2018).

54 R. Zhu et al., *A Social History of Middle Period China* (Cambridge, 2016).

55 N. Standen, 'Colouring Outside the Lines: Methods for a Global History of Eastern Eurasia, 600–1350', *TRHS*, 6th series, 29 (2019): 62.

56 For various provocative early modernist perspectives, see J.-P. Ghobrial, ed., *Global History and Microhistory* (Oxford, 2019).

57 E. Power, 'A Plea for the Middle Ages', *Economica* 5 (1922): 180.

58 Peter Schott, *Lucubratiunculae* (Strasbourg, 1497), fol. 116; translated in G. G. Coulton, *Life in the Middle Ages* (Cambridge, 1928), I, 242.

59 D. Dymond, 'God's Disputed Acre', *Journal of Ecclesiastical History* 50 (1999): 464–97.

60 M. Bakhtin, *Rabelais and His World* (Bloomington, 1984).

61 J. Delumeau, *Catholicisme entre Luther et Voltaire* (Paris, 1971).

62 J. Le Goff, *Time, Work and Culture in the Middle Ages* (Chicago, 1980); J.-C. Schmitt, 'Religion Populaire et Culture Folklorique', *Annales ESC* 31 (1976): 941–53.

63 J. van Engen, 'The Christian Middle Ages as an Historiographical Problem', *American Historical Review* 91 (1986): 519–52; in response, J.-C. Schmitt, 'Religion, Folklore, and Society in the Medieval West', in L. K. Little and B. H. Rosenwein, eds, *Debating the Middle Ages* (Oxford, 1998), 376–87.

64   R. Schnell, 'The Discourse on Marriage in the Middle Ages', *Speculum* 73 (1998): 771–86.

65   H. Grundmann, 'Litteratus-illitteratus', *Archiv für Kulturgeschichte* 40 (1958): 1–65, now translated in J. K. Deane, ed., *Herbert Grundmann (1902–1970): Essays on Heresy, Inquisition and Literacy* (York, 2019); M. Irvine, *The Making of Textual Culture* (Cambridge, 1994); M. T. Clanchy, *From Memory to Written Record*, 2nd edn (Oxford, 1993).

66   D. H. Green, 'Orality and Reading', *Speculum* 65 (1990): 267–80.

67   A. Gurevich, 'Oral and Written Culture of the Middle Ages', *New Literary History* 16 (1984): 51–66; J. M. H. Smith, 'Oral and Written: Saints, Miracles and Relics in Brittany *c*.850–1250', *Speculum* 65 (1990): 309–43; M. Innes, 'Memory, Orality and Literacy in an Early Medieval Society', *Past & Present* 158 (1998): 3–36.

68   R. Fletcher, *The Conversion of Europe* (London, 1997); P. Brown, *The Rise of Western Christendom*, 2nd edn (Oxford, 2003).

69   M. Camille, *Image on the Edge: The Margins of Medieval Art* (London, 1992).

70   R. McKitterick, ed., *Carolingian Culture* (Cambridge, 2003).

71   See also D. Crouch, *The Chivalric Turn: Conduct and Hegemony in Europe before 1300* (Oxford, 2019).

72   J. Baldwin, *Masters, Princes and Merchants: The Social Views of Peter the Chanter and His Circle*, 2 vols (Princeton, 1970); P. Biller, *The Measure of Multitude: Population in Medieval Thought* (Oxford, 2001).

73   H. Grundmann, *Religious Movements in the Middle Ages* (Notre Dame, 1995).

74   J.-C. Schmitt, *The Holy Greyhound* (Cambridge, 1983); M. G. Pegg, *The Corruption of Angels: The Great Inquisition of 1245–1246* (Princeton, 2001).

75   J. M. Bennett, 'Writing Fornication', *TRHS*, 6th series, 13 (2003): 131–62.

76   V. Reinburg, 'Liturgy and the Laity', *Sixteenth-Century Journal* 23 (1992): 529–32.

77   M. Goodich, 'The Politics of Canonization in the Thirteenth Century', *Church History* 44 (1975): 294–307; A. Kleinberg, *Prophets in Their Own Country: Living Saints and the Making of Sainthood in the Later Middle Ages* (Chicago, 1992).

78   L. A. Smoller, 'Defining the Boundaries of the Natural in Fifteenth-Century Brittany', *Viator* 28 (1997): 333–59.

79 R. Rusconi, *L'ordine dei peccati* (Bologna, 2002); A. Vauchez, ed., *Faire croire* (Rome, 1981).
80 W. C. Jordan, *The French Monarchy and the Jews from Philip Augustus to the Last Capetians* (Philadelphia, 1989).
81 J. B. Given, 'Chasing Phantoms: Philip IV and the Fantastic', in M. Frassetto, ed., *Heresy and the Persecuting Society in the Middle Ages* (Leiden, 2006), 273.
82 J. R. Strayer, *On the Medieval Origins of the Modern State* (Princeton, 1970).
83 Compare D. Barthélemy, *La Mutation de l'an mil a-t-elle eu lieu? Servage et chevalerie dans la France des Xe et XIe siècles* (Paris, 1997); T. Bisson, *The Crisis of the Twelfth Century* (Princeton, 2008).
84 C. Wickham, *Framing the Early Middle Ages* (Oxford, 2005), 56–150.
85 R. Bonney and W. M. Ormrod, eds, *Crises, Revolutions and Self-Sustained Growth* (Stanford, 1998).
86 S. R. Epstein, 'Town and Country', *Economic History Review* 46 (1993): 464.
87 P. Wormald, 'Germanic Power Structures', in L. Scales and O. Zimmer, *Power and the Nation in European History* (Cambridge, 2005), 105.
88 P. Freedman, *Images of the Medieval Peasant* (Stanford, 1999), 242, 38.
89 V. Groebner, 'Losing Face, Saving Face: Noses and Honour in the Late Medieval Town', *History Workshop Journal* 40 (1995): 1–15.
90 G. Halsall, ed., *Violence and Society in the Early Medieval West* (Woodbridge, 1998); R. Kaeuper, ed., *Violence in Medieval Society* (Woodbridge, 2000).
91 R. Weissmann, *Ritual Brotherhood in Renaissance Florence* (New York, 1982).
92 M. McLaughlin, *Consorting with Saints: Prayer for the Dead in Early Medieval France* (Ithaca, 1994), 176–7.
93 G. Koziol, 'England, France and the Problem of Sacrality in Twelfth-Century Ritual', in T. Bisson, ed. *Cultures of Power* (Philadelphia, 1995), 124–48; but see also N. Vincent, *The Holy Blood: King Henry III and the Westminster Blood Relic* (Cambridge, 2001), 186–201.
94 J. Nelson, 'Royal Saints and Early Medieval Kingship', *Studies in Church History* 10 (1973): 39–44; G. Klaniczay, *Holy Rulers and Blessed Princesses: Dynastic Cults in Medieval Central Europe* (Cambridge, 2002).
95 G. Ferzoco, *Il murale di Massa Marittima* (Leicester, 2005).

96   J. Gillingham, *The English in the Twelfth Century* (Woodbridge, 2000) and Patrick Wormald, 'Engla Lond: The Making of Allegiance', *Journal of Historical Sociology* 7 (1994): 1–24.

97   M. Innes, *State and Society in the Early Middle Ages* (Cambridge, 2000).

98   Smail, *Imaginary Cartographies*; G. L. Harriss, 'Political Society and the Growth of Government in Late Medieval England', *Past & Present* 138 (1993): 28–57; A. Musson and W. M. Ormrod, *The Evolution of English Justice* (Basingstoke, 1998).

99   S. K. Cohn, *The Lust for Liberty: The Politics of Social Revolt in Europe 1200–1425* (Cambridge, MA, 2006); D. A. Carpenter, 'English Peasants in Politics, 1258–1267', *Past & Present* 136 (1992): 3–42; C. Liddy, 'Urban Conflict in Late Fourteenth-Century England', *English Historical Review* 118 (2003): 1–32.

Chapter 5   Making and Remaking the Middle Ages

1   Quoted in Southern, 'Aspects of the European Tradition . . . IV', *TRHS*, 5th series, 23 (1973): 252.

2   R. W. Southern, *History and Historians*, ed. R. J. Bartlett (Oxford, 2004), 133.

3   O. G. Oexle, 'The Middle Ages through Modern Eyes', *TRHS*, 6th series, 9 (1999): 121–42.

4   S. Reynolds, 'The Idea of the Nation as a Political Community', in L. Scales and O. Zimmer, *Power and the Nation in European History* (Cambridge, 2005), 54–66.

5   D. Nirenberg, 'Mass Conversion and Genealogical Mentalities: Jews and Christians in Fifteenth-Century Spain', *Past & Present* 174 (2002): 3–41; S. A. Epstein, *Speaking of Slavery: Color, Ethnicity and Human Bondage in Italy* (Ithaca, 2001); S. Ahmed, 'Race as Sedimented History', *postmedieval: A Journal of Medieval Cultural Studies* 6 (2015). See also the other essays in that journal, and G. Heng, *The Invention of Race in the European Middle Ages* (Cambridge, 2018).

6   For various perspectives of this kind, see new afterword to F. Fukuyama, *The End of History and the Last Man* (London, 2006); R. Scruton, *The West and the Rest* (London, 2003); S. Huntingdon, *The Clash of Civilizations and the Remaking of the World Order* (New York, 1996).

7   For a sustained analysis of the deeper roots, see Matthew X.

Vernon, *The Black Middle Ages: Race and the Construction of the Middle Ages* (Basingstoke, 2018).

8 W. C. Jordan, 'Saving Medieval History', in J. van Engen, ed., *The Past and Future of Medieval Studies* (Notre Dame, 1994), 264–5; B. Holsinger, 'Medieval Studies, Postcolonial Studies, and the Genealogies of Critique', *Speculum* 77 (2002): 195–227; B. Holsinger, *The Premodern Condition* (Chicago, 2005).

9 J. C. Scott, *Domination and the Arts of Resistance* (Yale, 1992); C. Taylor, *Sources of the Self* (Harvard, 1992).

10 L. Zhang, *The River, the Plain, and the State: An Environmental Drama in Northern Song China, 1048–1128* (Cambridge, 2016); T. Johnson, *Law in Common: Legal Cultures in Late-Medieval England* (Oxford, 2020), Ch. 3.

11 M. Kestemont, V. Christlein and D. Stutzman, 'Artificial Paleography: Computational Approaches to Identifying Script Types in Medieval Manuscripts', *Speculum* 92 (2017).

12 For developments mainly in literary study, see K. Van Eickels, R. Weichselbaumer and I. Bennewitz, eds, *Mediaevistik und Neue Medien* (Ostfildern, 2004).

13 For early developments visible when the first edition of this book was written, see L. K. Little, 'Cypress Beams, Kufic Script and Cut Stone: Rebuilding the Master Narrative of European History', *Speculum* 79 (2004): 909–28; J. P. Arnason and B. Wittrock, eds, *Eurasian Transformations, Tenth to Thirteenth Centuries* (Leiden, 2004).

14 J. M. Bennett, 'Our Colleagues, Ourselves', in van Engen, ed., *The Past and Future of Medieval Studies*, 245–58.

15 J. R. Strayer, 'The Future of Medieval History', *Medievalia et Humanistica* n.s. 2 (1971): 179–88.

Further Reading

Chapter 1   Framing the Middle Ages

On medieval magic and its contexts, see R. Kieckhefer, *Magic in the Middle Ages* (Cambridge, 1989). Overviews of both medieval and medievalist historiography can be found in various general books, notably E. Breisach, *Historiography: Ancient, Medieval and Modern* (Chicago, 1983). Of particular, if highly idiosyncratic, interest is N. Cantor, *Inventing the Middle Ages* (Cambridge, 1991). An excellent introduction to academic and popular medievalisms old and new is given in M. Bull, *Thinking Medieval* (Houndmills, 2005); for US perspectives see J. van Engen, ed., *The Past and Future of Medieval Studies* (Notre Dame, 1994). For one sense of how the academy has changed, see J. Chance, ed., *Women Medievalists and the Academy* (Madison, 2005).

There are many general textbooks: for the early period see M. Innes, *An Introduction to Early Medieval Western Europe* (London, 2007) and J. M. H. Smith, *Europe After Rome: A New Cultural History 500–1000* (Oxford, 2005); for the central middle ages, J. H. Mundy, *Europe in the High Middle Ages* (New York, 1973) and M. Barber, *The Two Cities: Medieval Europe 1050–1320* (London, 1993); and for the late middle ages, see Charles F. Briggs, *The Body Broken*, 2nd edn (Abingdon, 2020). Two sparkling works on England supply wider thematic dividends: M. T. Clanchy,

England and its Rulers, 1066–1272, 3rd edn (Oxford, 2006) and R. Horrox and W. M. Ormrod, eds, *A Social History of England 1200–1500* (2006). P. Linehan and J. Nelson, eds, *The Medieval World* (London, 2003) is a fascinating collection of articles, and C. Wickham, *Medieval Europe* (New Haven, 2016) a provocative and panoramic overview.

Chapter 2   Tracing the Middle Ages

A selection of sources on the 1381 revolt is collected in R. B. Dobson, ed. and trans., *The Peasants' Revolt of 1381,* 2nd edn (Houndmills, 1983); for European comparators, see S. K. Cohn, ed. and trans., *Popular Protest in Late Medieval Europe* (Manchester, 2004). There are many general source collections and translation editions; one might note in particular those published in the series *Oxford Medieval Texts, Manchester Medieval Sources,* and Broadview Press's *Readings in Medieval Civilizations and Cultures.* For particular genres see the series *Typologie des sources du Moyen Age,* some of which are wholly or partly in English, e.g. B. Kienzle, ed., *The Sermon* (Turnhout, 2000). R. C. van Caenegem, *Guide to the Sources of Medieval History* (Amsterdam, 1978) is a bit old-fashioned, but still helpful. On issues of women and medieval sources, see J. T. Rosenthal, ed., *Medieval Women and the Sources of Medieval History* (Athens, GA, 1990).

For English research, E. A. Gooder, *Latin for Local History: An Introduction* (Harlow, 1978) is very useful for manorial records, R. E. Latham, *Revised Medieval Latin Wordlist* (Oxford, 1965) is a handy addition to classical Latin dictionaries and, for guides to palaeographic detail, see C. Trice Martin, *The Record Interpreter* (Chichester, 1982) and A. Cappelli, *Dizionario di abbreviature latine ed italiane,* 2nd edn (Milan, 1929; reprint 1990).

For a variety of cases and viewpoints, see K. Heidecker, ed., *Charters and the Use of the Written Word in Medieval Society* (Turnhout, 2000), and a brilliant analysis of early medieval evidence is G. Koziol, *The Politics of Memory and Identity in Carolingian Royal Diplomas* (Turnhout, 2012); F. Curta, 'Merovingian and Carolingian Gift-Giving', *Speculum* 81

(2006): 671–99, provides a helpful survey of approaches to gift exchange; for later periods, see V. Groebner, *Liquid Assets, Dangerous Gifts* (Philadelphia, 2002). For a general introduction to chronicles, see B. Smalley, *Historians of the Middle Ages* (London, 1974); particular studies appear in the ongoing annual yearbook, The *Medieval Chronicle* (Amsterdam, 1999–). Most important for England is A. Gransden, *Historical Writing in England*, 2 vols (London, 1974–82); see also C. Given-Wilson, *Chronicles* (London, 2004). Legal sources have no general introduction as such, but useful issues are raised in M. Goodich, ed., *Voices from the Bench* (Houndmills, 2006), and T. Dean, *Crime in Medieval Europe* (Harlow, 2001) is an excellent guide to the subject area. Two good introductions to medieval art are M. Camille, *Gothic Art* (London, 1996) and V. Sekules, *Medieval Art* (Oxford, 2001).

Chapter 3   Reading the Middle Ages

P. Burke, *History and Social Theory*, 3rd edn (Cambridge, 2005) provides a guide to anthropological approaches, among other things, and P. Monaghan, *Social and Cultural Anthropology: A Very Short Introduction* (Oxford, 2000) gives a quick way into the discipline. Four works particularly influential on medievalists are E. Durkheim, *The Elementary Forms of the Religious Life* (London, 1915), M. Douglas, *Purity and Danger* (London, 1966), V. Turner, *The Ritual Process* (Chicago, 1969), and P. Bourdieu, *Outline of a Theory of Practice* (Cambridge, 1977). Essential for understanding medieval literacy is M. T. Clanchy, *From Memory to Written Record*, 2nd edn (Oxford, 1993).

An excellent guide to statistical analysis is given by P. Hudson, *History by Numbers* (London, 2000), and a clear discussion and critique of economic theories pertaining to the medieval period in J. Hatcher and M. Bailey, *Modelling the Middle Ages* (Oxford, 2001). The early medieval economy is analysed magisterially and controversially in M. McCormick, *Origins of the European Economy* (Cambridge, 2001), a book discussed in *Early Medieval Europe* 12 (2003). Nothing as synoptic exists for the later period, but see D. Wood,

Medieval Economic Thought (Cambridge, 2002) and R. H. Britnell, *The Commercialization of English Society, 1000–1500* (Cambridge, 1993).

There are various guides to archaeology and its theories, such as P. Bahn, *Archaeology: A Very Short Introduction*, 2nd edn (Oxford, 2000) and I. Hodder, *Archaeological Theory Today*, 2nd edn (Cambridge, 2012). Specifically on the medieval period, see C. Gerrard, *Medieval Archaeology* (London, 2003). On castles, addressing the issues raised here, see R. Liddiard, *Castles in Context* (Macclesfield, 2005); for burial practices, G. Halsall, *Early Medieval Cemeteries* (Glasgow, 1995) and the review article by T. Dickenson in *Early Medieval Europe* 11 (2002). Also interesting is R. Gilchrist, *Gender and Archaeology* (London, 1999). There is as yet no very easy introduction to the highly technical scientific work on historical DNA analysis and the like, but see volume 4 of the journal *Medieval Worlds*, on 'The Genetic Challenge to Medieval History and Archaeology', and M. H. Green, ed., *Pandemic Disease in the Medieval World: Rethinking the Black Death* (Kalamazoo, 2015). Reading a variety of relevant journal articles fairly quickly allows one a sense of how they present their material and their findings, and thus how to interpret (though perhaps not critique) them as a layperson. On climate and medieval history, see B. M. S. Campbell, *The Great Transition* (Cambridge, 2016) and R. Hoffmann, *An Environmental History of Medieval Europe* (Cambridge, 2014).

Literary theory plays an influential role in N. Partner, ed., *Writing Medieval History* (London, 2005) and the chapters there by Murray and Beattie offer excellent analyses of medieval gender and sexuality. See also R. M. Karras, *From Boys to Men* (Philadelphia, 2002), R. M. Karras, *Sexuality in Medieval Europe* (London, 2005) and M. Erler and M. Kowaleski, eds, *Gendering the Master Narrative: Women and Power in the Middle Ages* (Ithaca, 2003). An excellent discussion of theoretical issues by an historian of late antiquity is E. A. Clark, *History, Theory, Text: Historians and the Linguistic Turn* (Cambridge, MA, 2004). Joel T. Rosenthal usefully discusses the narrative elements of various sources in *Telling Tales: Sources and Narration in Late Medieval England* (University Park, PA, 2003).

Chapter 4   Debating the Middle Ages

On ritual, see E. Muir, *Ritual in Early Modern Europe* (Cambridge, 1997) and G. Koziol, *Begging Pardon and Favor* (Ithaca, 1992), particularly pp. 289–324. A critique of the concept for medievalists was launched by P. Buc, *The Dangers of Ritual* (Princeton, 2001), and a trenchant reply given in Koziol, 'The Dangers of Polemic', *Early Medieval Europe* 11 (2002): 367–88. C. Humphrey, *The Politics of Carnival* (Manchester, 2001) presents a concise and insightful discussion of rebellion in the context of ritual.

Various key articles on 'feudalism' are reproduced in L. K. Little and B. H. Rosenwein, eds, *Debating the Middle Ages* (Oxford, 1998); see also S. Reynolds, *Fiefs and Vassals* (Oxford, 1994) and subsequent reviews. Probably the most important recent work is C. West, *Reframing the Feudal Revolution* (Cambridge, 2013). An interesting take on social structures from several different perspectives is given by S. Rigby, *English Society in the Later Middle Ages: Class, Status and Gender* (London, 1995). Two key works exploring 'two cultures' models are J. Le Goff, *Time, Work and Culture in the Middle Ages* (Chicago, 1980) and A. Gurevich, *Medieval Popular Culture* (Cambridge, 1988); for a different view, see J. van Engen, 'The Christian Middle Ages as an Historiographical Problem', *American Historical Review* 91 (1986) and E. Duffy, *The Stripping of the Altars* (Yale, 1992). On ordinary lay people's relationship(s) with religion, see J. H. Arnold, *Belief and Unbelief in Medieval Europe* (London, 2005).

Global approaches to the middle ages are still at a relatively early stage of debate and discussion, but for a prescient attempt to represent the period not only through Europe but the world, see R. McKitterick, ed., *Atlas of the Medieval World* (Oxford, 2004). C. Holmes and N. Standen, eds, *The Global Middle Ages* (Oxford, 2018), a *Past & Present Supplement* volume, was a main point of entry for my own understanding of the topic, and the journal *Medieval Worlds* provides a number of extremely interesting articles. J. Belich et al., eds, *The Prospect of Global History* (Oxford, 2016) contains several chapters that serve as both introduction and challenge.

Power is a topic much debated, and wonderfully framed by Tim Reuter in the posthumous collection of his essays, *Medieval Polities and Modern Mentalities*, ed. J. L. Nelson (Cambridge, 2006). To pick just a few works of interest, for the early period, see particularly M. Innes, *State and Society in the Early Middle Ages* (Cambridge, 2000) and C. Wickham, *Framing the Early Middle Ages* (Oxford, 2005), and for later periods W. M. Ormrod, *Political Life in Medieval England* (Basingstoke, 1995), D. Nirenberg, *Communities of Violence* (Princeton, 1997) and J. Watts, *Henry VI and the Politics of Kingship* (Cambridge, 1996). The case for and against the medieval 'state' was the focus of keen discussion between R. Rees Davies and Susan Reynolds in *Journal of Historical Sociology* 16 (2003).

Chapter 5   Making and Remaking the Middle Ages

On modern uses of the medieval, again see M. Bull, *Thinking Medieval* (Houndmills, 2005), and for an area of current debate, B. Holsinger, *Neomedievalism, Neoconservatism, and the War on Terror* (Chicago, 2007). The medievalness of Europe is set out in R. Bartlett, *The Making of Europe* (London, 1993) and J. Le Goff, *The Birth of Europe* (Oxford, 2005), and given a particular modern importance in P. J. Geary, *The Myth of Nations* (Princeton, 2002). The political importance of *la longue durée* for feminism – and implicitly for much else – is strongly argued in J. M. Bennett, *History Matters: Patriarchy and the Challenge of Feminism* (Philadelphia, 2006).

Index